A GLANCE AT WHAT ideaSELLERS
are saying INSIDE THIS BOOK:

"Too often we feel compelled to present every thread of our research, and in the process, we lose our focus. And if we lose focus, we lose the client." Cathy Austin, LOOP9 MARKETING, page 21

"Going into a presentation with the spark of something—and letting the group contribute to the energy of the idea and make it their own—is almost always more successful for us." Trish Berrong, HALLMARK CARDS, page 38

"I have watched parades of creative people destroy their own work—after the client finally buys into their ideas. They blab themselves right out of a client's approval. If they finally say yes, then say thank you—and leave the room with your idea sold." Brian Collins, COLLINS DESIGN, page 201

"If you choose to use theatrics in client presentations, my advice is to make it personal, make it memorable and leave with a laugh, often at your own expense." Marc English, MARC ENGLISH DESIGN, page 193

"A great presentation will give the client all the tools he or she needs to then turn around and sell the idea internally." Sally Hogshead, AUTHOR AND COPYWRITER, page 47

"It's OK to sometimes say 'no' or 'I don't know.' Creative people get into the most trouble by promising what they can't deliver or by trying to give an answer when they don't have one." Jeff Long, DIGITAL KITCHEN, page 220

"Nothing replaces practice, even if you're a natural-born salesperson. There's a difference between knowing what you've created and knowing how to sell it." Don McNeill, DIGITAL KITCHEN, page 90

"By using stories in presentations, we're enticing people to follow along. Stories say come this way, take that hill, believe in something better." Lisa Maulhardt, STONE YAMASHITA PARTNERS, page 167

"We not only have to speak the language of business, we have to know that business. If we really want to sell an idea, we have to saturate ourselves, immerse ourselves and know what these things mean to the client's customers." Stefan Mumaw, REIGN AGENCY, page 23

"Too many presentations look like they have been put together by lawyers. The presenter takes all the reason why a client should buy and lists them, hoping one will hit a homerun. It seldom works. The secret of a good presentation is sacrifice." Al Ries, RIES AND RIES, page 131

"If they feel they birthed it, they can't kill it. If you truly collaborate with your client, there's a good chance you'll sell your strongest ideas without having them watered down." David Schimmel, AND PARTNERS, page 37

"When presenting, we work to create an experience and help clients visualize ideas as reality." DJ Stout, PENTAGRAM DESIGN, page 130

"The more you pitch, the more you learn to make sure the right ideas are right for the client and the product you're pitching. You have to believe in what you're doing and not get bitter." Jakob Trollbäck, TROLLBÄCK + COMPANY, page 3

ideaSELLING

SUCCESSFULLY PITCH YOUR
CREATIVE IDEAS TO BOSSES, CLIENTS
AND OTHER DECISION MAKERS

Sam Harrison

HOW
BOOKS

Cincinnati, Ohio
WWW.HOWDESIGN.COM

For more excellent books and resources for designers, visit www.howdesign.com.

14 13 12 11 10   5 4 3 2 1

Distributed in Canada by Fraser Direct
100 Armstrong Avenue
Georgetown, Ontario, Canada L7G 5S4
Tel: (905) 877-4411

Distributed in the U.K. and Europe by David & Charles
Brunel House, Newton Abbot, Devon, TQ12 4PU, England
Tel: (+44) 1626-323200, Fax: (+44) 1626-323319
E-mail: postmaster@davidandcharles.co.uk

Distributed in Australia by Capricorn Link
P.O. Box 704, Windsor, NSW 2756 Australia
Tel: (02) 4577-3555

The cataloging-in-publication data for this book can be found on record at the Library of Congress.

EDITED BY amy schell owen
DESIGNED BY grace ring (BASED ON A DESIGN BY KARLA BAKER)
PRODUCTION COORDINATED BY greg nock

media

To Hope, world's best salesperson.

about the author.

Sam Harrison has successfully pitched ideas for more than twenty years in creative agency, corporate, free-lance and consulting roles. He was a senior vice president of creative services and branding for an S&P 500 company and has worked with such clients and associates as NFL, Major League Baseball, Hallmark, Hasbro and John Denver Environmental Groups.

© Greg Newington, www.newingtonphotography.com

He provides creativity-related talks, seminars and coaching to agencies, firms and associations throughout North America and beyond. He also teaches creativity, idea-pitching and writing classes at Portfolio Center's graduate studies program.

He is the author of *IdeaSpotting: How to Find Your Next Great Idea* and *Zing! Five Steps and 101 Tips for Creativity on Command.*

He can be reached at www.zingzone.com and sdh@mindspring.com.

SELLING BRINGS IDEAS TO *life.*

My first book, *Zing!*, introduced a five-step method for generating ideas. Here's how that process looks:

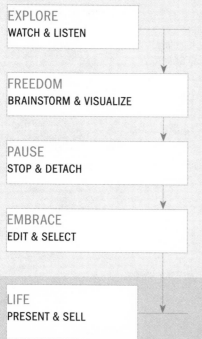

EXPLORE
WATCH & LISTEN

My second book, *IdeaSpotting*, focused on this first step of exploring for insights and associations as fuel for ideas.

FREEDOM
BRAINSTORM & VISUALIZE

PAUSE
STOP & DETACH

EMBRACE
EDIT & SELECT

LIFE
PRESENT & SELL

IdeaSelling focuses on the Life phase of the creative process—bringing ideas to life by successfully presenting and selling them to decision makers.

table
OF CONTENTS

"It's useless to be a creative, original thinker unless you can also sell what you create.

Management cannot be expected to recognize a good idea unless it's presented to them by a good sales person."

—David Ogilvy, ADVERTISING PIONEER

"There's no correlation between how good your idea is and how likely your organization will be to embrace it. None. It's not about good ideas. It's about selling those ideas and making them happen. If you're failing to get things done, it's not because your ideas suck. It's because you don't know how to sell them."

—Seth Godin, MARKETING EXPERT

"Everyone lives by selling something."

—Robert Louis Stevenson, NOVELIST AND POET

IT'S NOT ENOUGH TO HAVE IDEAS.
You also have to sell those ideas.

Having ideas slammed down and stomped dead is the very definition of No Fun. Idea rejection makes us sad, mad and crazy enough to gnaw on tree trunks and laugh hysterically at inappropriate times.

We scream to rafters about how clients "just don't get it." We rave about how our ideas would make it to the finish line if we only had more time, more money or more creative decision makers.

The problem, however, isn't decision makers, budgets or time. The problem is our selling skills. We know all about how to generate ideas. We don't know nearly enough about how to sell those ideas.

But shouldn't good ideas stand on their own? Shouldn't they sell themselves? Not a chance. In fact, the better and bolder the ideas, the more they need selling. Because they're different. Challenging. Risky. They insist people

let go of their old ideas to grab your new ideas. Selling helps that happen.

In this book are tips, techniques and thoughts to assist in selling ideas to decision makers. Some insights come from my years of successfully pitching concepts to decision makers at NFL, Major League Baseball, Hallmark, Merrill Lynch, John Denver Environmental Groups and other organizations.

Some tips come from designers, writers, architects and others in creative roles. And still more techniques come from selling gurus and professional salespeople.

The book's content is offered in bite-size doses, making it easy to read and review. Start at the beginning, the middle or the end. Just start somewhere. And you'll soon start selling more ideas.

Playing the victim.

"They just don't get it."

"She wouldn't recognize a good idea if it walked up and asked her to dance."

"It's impossible to sell something creative to somebody who's not creative."

Ever used these lines after having ideas pushed back by decision makers? Sure. Most of us have hidden behind these excuses and others at down-and-out times.

But they're wasted words. Whimpers. Cop-outs. Because we're responsible for presenting ideas in ways that connect with decision makers. Address their wants and needs. Help them appreciate benefits and values.

"Don't rely on the client to connect the dots," David Schimmel, And Partners founder and creative director, tells his team members. "That's our job."

EACH TIME WE FALL BACK ON THE THEY-DON'T-GET-IT EXCUSE, WE LABEL OURSELVES VICTIMS. AND VICTIMS ARE POWERLESS.

NOT PLAYING
the victim.

"We've given excellent pitches that weren't picked for one reason or another," says Jakob Trollbäck, founder and creative director of Trollbäck + Company.

"For example, a client might come to us and scream 'blue sky, blue sky—do whatever you want to do,'" he says. "They tell us they want something revolutionary, so we pitch that. And then we find out they're really more conservative than they thought."

Pitches are lost for a reason, Trollbäck adds, and the important thing is to figure out why you lost. "The more you do this," he says, "the more you learn to make sure the great ideas are right for the client and product you're pitching.

"You have to believe in what you're doing and not get bitter. If you let it harden you, you're going to just get old and dull."

3

1

HOW TO DEAL WITH
DECISION MAKERS.

"I have learned to respect ideas wherever they
come from. Often they come from clients."

—Leo Burnett, ADVERTISING PIONEER

It's not about you.

Decision makers aren't interested in your pain.

THEY'RE INTERESTED IN *THEIR* PAIN.

They want to know how your idea will ease their pain.
Solve their problem. Provide worry-free sleep.

Or maybe they want to know how the idea will make
their lives fun and joyful. Make them prosperous.
Make life easier.

The last thing they want to hear are your problems.
The overtime you put into the idea. Your hassles along
the way. Your sleepless nights and supreme sacrifices.

Don't whine or complain during your pitch.
Keep it positive.

STAY OUT OF YOUR PROBLEMS.
STAY IN THEIR SOLUTIONS.

"The world doesn't want to hear about the labor pains. They just want to see the baby."

—Johnny Sain, BASEBALL PITCHER

FEEL THEIR *pain.*

"No pain, no gain" has significance when selling ideas. Because in many cases, if there's not some pain, there'll be no sale.

Luckily for us, the pain resides on the other side of the table—with the decision maker. The pain may be a problem she's tackling. A situation she's facing. A change she's making.

"Take time to find out your client's deeper fears," says Sally Hogshead, award-winning copywriter and author of *Fascinate*, "the ones you can only learn from trusted conversations."

The decision maker may not always recognize the cause of her discomfort, so it's up to you to identify the source. And to present ideas to alleviate pain.

EYES, EARS,
fears.

Communicate with decision makers through their eyes, ears and fears.

GIVE DECISION MAKERS
A BREAK.

We often get our pants in a wad when clients ask stupid questions, don't grasp concepts and won't make quick decisions. Why can't they just say OK, dammit?

But think back to the last time someone was selling you something. Maybe an article of clothing. A piece of furniture. A new car or computer.

Chances are, you didn't jump straight to go. You probably hesitated. Asked dumb questions. Flip-flopped between the red one and the blue one. Compared apples and oranges, then asked about kumquats.

Maybe you said something like, "Well, I sort of like this one, but this is nice too... do you have anything in-between? Or maybe I'll just wait a few days... you know, see what else is out there..."

SELLING IS HARD, BUT SO IS BUYING. THERE'S MONEY ON THE LINE. PRESSURE. EGO.

SO GIVE DECISION MAKERS A BREAK. THEY'RE BUYERS, JUST LIKE THE REST OF US.

PLACE YOUR LADDER
on the right wall.

Climbing a ladder doesn't make much sense if your ladder is on the wrong wall, points out leadership expert Stephen Covey. Likewise, having ideas is praiseworthy but usually senseless if they don't meet objectives.

At the start of projects, write out strategies and shout about objectives. Creative briefs are widely used, but they are seldom maximized, says Brian Collins, owner and creative director of COLLINS:, a design and brand consultancy.

"Unfortunately, most creative briefs are neither creative nor brief," he says. "They wind up being pre-chewed marketing drivel. Without a great brief to navigate the journey, a creative team will be dancing on the deck of the Titanic."

Collins suggests writing a mission that reframes the opportunity as big as possible and in such as way that it could change the world.

"Get specific about what you want to make happen," he says. "What do you want the audience to believe? To feel? To remember? How will you convince them? Write it down and then edit. And keep editing until your brief is as sharp, clean and lethal as a razor."

sign here, *please.*

In addition to creative briefs, I've sometimes used a simple objectives sheet:

DATE:

PROJECT:

OUR PRIMARY OBJECTIVES FOR THIS PROJECT ARE:

signature   signature

The purpose? To make sure the client and I clarify and agree on objectives—well before the team generates ideas and concepts. Note the two signature lines—one for me, one for the client.

This easy sheet helps keep work on track, and it is often an idea saver during presentations. When the client raises vague objections, out comes the signed objectives sheet to help refocus discussions.

Objectives often trump objections!

WHERE IS YOUR DECISION MAKER
SITTING ON *the buyer's bench?*

When you present an idea, your decision maker sits on a Buyer's Bench like this:

| UNAWARE | AWARE | UNDERSTAND | ACCEPT | BUY |

Your decision maker may be UNAWARE of the concept.

Or she may be AWARE of the concept but doesn't understand it.

Or she may UNDERSTAND but isn't ready to accept.

Or she may ACCEPT the idea's value but needs nudging to commit and BUY.

The iPod was introduced in 2001, but at that time only rabid techies and early adopters were to the far right on the Buyer's Bench. Most of us were in the neighborhood of Unaware or Aware when it came to portable digital players. Gradually informed and persuaded by ads, articles and friends, we slowly slid down the bench and became Buyers.

Before you present an idea, determine your decision maker's place on the Buyer's Bench. If she already understands the concept and is leaning toward acceptance, odds are up for making the sale in one pitch.

If she is vaguely aware of the concept—or totally unaware—you may need conversations and multiple presentations, perhaps supplemented by education, to move her toward buy-in.

BUYER'S BENCH

Before pitching, locate your decision maker's position on a Buyer's Bench.

PROJECT/IDEA:
DECISION MAKER:

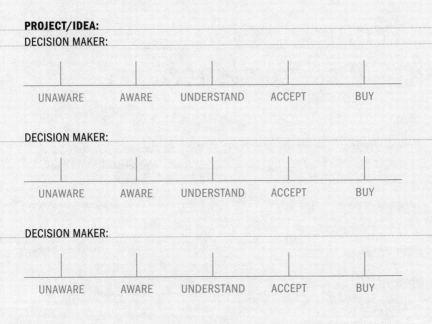

UNAWARE AWARE UNDERSTAND ACCEPT BUY

DECISION MAKER:

UNAWARE AWARE UNDERSTAND ACCEPT BUY

DECISION MAKER:

UNAWARE AWARE UNDERSTAND ACCEPT BUY

FOUR Cs

OF *excellence.*

Any artistic endeavor—a film, play, novel, painting or other creative effort—rises to excellence when it possesses:

CLARITY

The artist knows where she's taking you and it shows, even if the piece is complex or ambiguous.

CONTENT

Evidence of forethought and substance.

CREATIVITY

Originality and value.

CRAFT

Shape, form, flow and other reflections of professionalism.

Many entertaining and rewarding creations possess two or three of these Cs. Excellence demands all four.

Use the Four Cs to evaluate your ideas:

DOES THE IDEA CLEARLY MEET A NEED OR SOLVE A PROBLEM?

DOES IT HAVE SUBSTANCE?

IS IT ORIGINAL AND VALUABLE FOR YOUR AUDIENCE?

IS IT PROFESSIONALLY CRAFTED?

If you can answer yes to these four questions, you'll walk in with an excellent idea. If you can't answer yes, consider refinements.

Value your ideas.

Know your idea's cost, but also know its value.

INSTEAD OF FOCUSING ON FEATURES, FLAUNT BENEFITS.

What's the idea's true value to your decision maker? Does it solve a problem? Save time? Earn money? Recognize employees? Satisfy customers? Attract prospects? Provide other tangible payback?

When you know the idea's value, you have a head start. You've come to solve a problem. To give rather than take. To help rather than hassle. To advise rather than sell.

"The word 'selling' doesn't enter my brain," says Jeff Long, creative director at Digital Kitchen. "I want to be a partner with the client, an adviser."

"WHY SHOULD I care?"

One way to test an idea's value is by imaging yourself as the decision maker and asking, "Why should I care?" Your answers will articulate value. And if you don't have strong answers? Well...

RISKS *and* REWARDS.

One freezing February night, my wife and I arrived at the Olympic training facility in Park City, Utah, to go down the Olympic bobsled run.

Hope took one look at the stark, icy course rising high into the dark sky and said, "It'll take rope and ether to get me on that thing." I shared her uneasiness. And misgivings multiplied as we scanned a stack of injury waivers awaiting our signatures.

Only when we met the pro racer who would steer our bobsled did we start to relax. He carefully explained his plan and our roles. And as he described the thrills of racing down seventeen curves at five Gs, adventurous grins took over our faces.

We lifted pens and signed waivers. Rewards outweighed risks.

Each time you present an idea, a decision maker sits across from you weighing risks. If rewards are higher than risks, chances are good for acceptance. If dangers exceed dividends, it's likely a lost cause.

Raise potential rewards, reduce potential risks.

REDUCE RISKS,
raise rewards.

Most risk-reducing or reward-raising happens prior to pitches. You step back and stare at your idea, seeking ways to make it more rewarding or less risky for decision makers.

But by anticipating your decision maker's thought process, you can also shift risk-reward ratios during your pitch. For example:

DECISION MAKER THINKS:
"My boss is going to go ballistic over the cost of this..."

YOUR RISK-REDUCING STATEMENT:
"I know the numbers might be a hard sell when you show the budget to Brian, so we've calculated the return on investment..."

DECISION MAKER THINKS:
"I'll never be able to explain this idea to the board..."

YOUR RISK-REDUCING STATEMENT:
"By the way, Meredith, we've created an eight-minute presentation—complete with video overview—for you to take to the board meeting..."

DECISION MAKER THINKS:
"This idea is going to suck up weeks of my team's time..."

YOUR RISK-REDUCING STATEMENT:
"I know this looks like an overwhelming project, William, but we'll implement in stages and cheaply outsource much of the grunt work..."

FROM *don't* TO *do.*

Sometimes you can use the word "don't" to influence the decision maker's thoughts and reduce risks in her mind.

As master magician Steve Cohen points out in *Win the Crowd*, there's a "don't/unless" pattern we can use to persuade people:

DON'T
UNLESS

For example:

"Don't say yes on this unless you're really sure."

"Don't go with this idea unless you're ready to expand your services."

"Don't decide now unless this is an idea you could enjoy living with."

As Cohen points out, the opposite meaning is strongly expressed in these sentences. When you say "don't," the decision maker thinks, "why not?" Then after the word "unless," you provide subtle justification.

This isn't for pathologically indecisive clients—offering lines like these would only provide cover for their delays. But the don't/unless pattern can nudge people who aren't quick decision makers but like to think they are.

Avoid infomercial-like bluster. ("Don't say yes to this idea unless you're ready to quadruple your customer base and travel the world in your private jet...") Be honest with enticements.

DON'T/UNLESS *trial.*

Think of three "don't/unless" sentences for the next time you need to reduce risks during a meeting with decision makers.

But don't try this unless you want to work magic.

DON'T

UNLESS

DON'T

UNLESS

DON'T

UNLESS

HOLD UP
your homework.

Ideas appear less risky as decision makers realize you've researched the situation. To show you've done your homework, ask a few questions:

"While researching past recruiting efforts, I saw that two years ago the company reached out to smaller colleges. What are your thoughts about that effort?"

"I noticed both major competitors include video clips on their websites. Are there reasons that hasn't been tried here?"

"For three years now, attendance and donations dipped during the third quarter. Why do you think that happens each year?"

Of course, know when to stop waving your research.

"Remember that you won't persuade by showing how much you know," says sales adviser Jim Cathcart. "Persuasion takes place when they see you as a solution to the challenges they care about."

LOSE FOCUS,

LOSE CLIENT.

"THE MOST EFFECTIVE PRESENTATIONS ARE THOSE WHERE YOU GIVE JUST ENOUGH RESEARCH TO SET THE STAGE FOR YOUR IDEA," SAYS CATHY AUSTIN, PRINCIPAL OF LOOP9 MARKETING.

She points to a scene in the film *Nothing in Common* as a glowing example.

"Tom Hanks plays a creative director pitching an ad campaign to an airline executive," she says. "He walks in and says something like: 'Our research shows you've captured the business traveler. Where there's room for improvement is with the family trade. Picture this...' And he launches his presentation.

"It's a beautiful pitch, because his setup says 'we did our research' without going into all the details. Too often I think we feel compelled to present every thread of our research, and in the process, we lose our focus.

"And if we lose focus, we lose the client."

Speak the language *of business.*

Make your presentations energetic and fun. Add drama. Tug at heartstrings. Share yourself.

But don't forget every pitch is a business proposition. It's OK to dazzle decision makers with jaw-dropping designs and breathtaking copy. But you won't get go-aheads without getting down to business.

And that means speaking the language of business.

No need to be a Warren Buffett, Anne Mulcahy or Michael Porter. Just know the basics of profit and loss. Understand principles of marketing and branding. Appreciate the difference between strategies and tactics.

How do you learn this stuff? Take a class or two at a community college. Read a few business books. Listen to interviews with business leaders. Ask questions to business-centric friends and relatives.

DECISION MAKERS ARE AFTER YOUR CREATIVE IDEAS AND DON'T EXPECT YOU TO HOLD AN MBA. THEY HAVE A PASSEL OF THOSE TYPES WITHIN SLAPPING DISTANCE.

They do, however, want to know why they should spend money on your ideas. And that means talking their language and knowing their business.

KNOW THE business.

"We not only have to speak the language of business, we have to know that business," says Stefan Mumaw, author of *Caffeine for the Creative Team* and creative director at Reign Agency.

Just tossing around a few business terms isn't enough. "If we really want to sell an idea," says Mumaw, "we have to saturate ourselves with the industry, immerse ourselves in the product or service and know what these things mean to the client's customers."

Mumaw tells of pitching an idea to a manufacturer of DJ equipment, an industry he knew absolutely nothing about. "But a few folks in our brainstorming session were deeply entrenched in that culture," he says, "and the best ideas were coming from them.

"I quickly saw our best shot for selling these ideas would be to include those people with personal experience in our presentation. We brought them into the meeting, and, with their own gruff, street-talk way, they sold the client.

"It wasn't just the language of that business. It was also the knowledge of the business."

Personality *plus.*

You could cover a psychiatrist's couch with all the tests for detecting personality types. And salespeople borrow from such tests—Myers-Briggs, Birkman and others—to help profile decision makers.

One method I find helpful on an admittedly elementary level is the DISC model. Developed by Dr. William Marston in the 1920s, DISC uses four quadrants to classify behavior.

DISC is an acronym for:

DOMINANCE—demanding and decisive

INFLUENCE—social and talkative

STEADINESS—thoughtful and steady

COMPLIANCE—cautious and systematic

By observing work styles and personal traits of decision makers, you can use DISC to loosely peg basic personality types. Dr. Marston would likely flip in his grave over such scant evaluations. But, with practice, you'll find clues on how to present to and interact with D-Types, I-Types, S-Types and C-Types.

"Every pitch is a chemistry test—testing the chemistry between the decision maker and the person presenting the idea."

—Don McNeill, PRESIDENT OF DIGITAL KITCHEN

D-TYPE
DECISION MAKERS.

DOMINANCE

Extroverted. Active. Demanding. Forceful. Egocentric. Aggressive. Decisive.

CEOs often fall in this quadrant.

When selling to D-Types:

Let them know they're important and that you value their time. Trim fluff. Link emotional elements directly to strategy and benefits. Be prepared for blunt questions and quick decisions.

"Show me a guy who thinks he's a self-made man, and I"ll show you the easiest sell in the world. All you have to do is make him think it's his idea."

—Harvey Mackay, AUTHOR AND SPEAKER

I-TYPE
DECISION MAKERS.

INFLUENCE

*Extroverted. Active. Social. Talkative. Emotional.
Optimistic. Warm. Convincing. Magnetic. Trusting.*

Sales and marketing people often fit this quadrant.

When selling to I-Types:

Involve them in your presentation with conversations,
questions and interactions. Include storytelling and
emotional tugs. Stay positive and upbeat. Be prepared
for interruptions, questions and comments.

"If you're speaking and not getting a reaction,
well, you are just making a speech."

—Bill Clinton, FORMER U.S. PRESIDENT

S-TYPE
DECISION MAKERS.

STEADINESS

Introverted. Calm. Relaxed. Deliberate. Consistent. Concerned for employees and family. Uncomfortable with sudden change.

Human resources people are often in this quadrant.

When selling to S-Types:

Involve these decision makers in your presentation. The more radical the idea, the more you'll need to reassure. Show how the idea will benefit employees and other stakeholders, and how it will be painlessly rolled out to those audiences.

"Any change, even a change for the better, is always accompanied by drawbacks and discomforts."
—Arnold Bennett, WRITER

C-TYPE
DECISION MAKERS.

COMPLIANCE

Introverted. Cautious. Systematic. Accurate. Comfortable with rules, regulations and structure.

Accounting and purchasing people often fall in this quadrant.

When selling to C-Types:

Cling close to facts. Limit fluff. Emotional elements must directly relate to strategy, process, revenue gains and cost savings. Let them know you appreciate quality work and the value of doing it right the first time. Shower them with details and follow-up.

"The reason Apple is really good, I think, and the reason stores succeeded, is not just because we know the big idea, but we have a real passion for the littlest detail."

—Ron Johnson, APPLE COMPUTER
SENIOR VICE PRESIDENT

DISC *quadrants.*

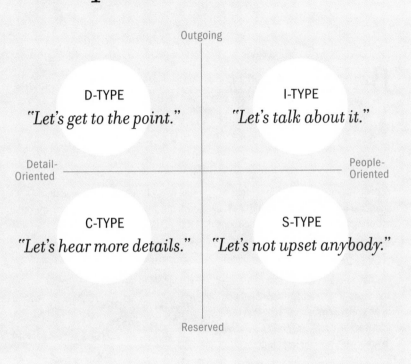

CAVEATS:

1. Applying DISC by observation only and without testing subjects is simply a low-grade technique for gaining general opinions of personality types—don't overplay its significance.

2. Few people fit completely in any one quadrant. Primary traits may point toward a particular personality type, but the person may also possess traits of one or more other types. Pay attention to all traits when preparing presentations.

Bonded *yet*?

Economist and writer Ben Stein tells of going car shopping with a friend. As they sat down with a saleswoman, the friend quickly confessed he had made mistakes in life and his credit was a mess.

The saleswoman looked him in the eyes and said, "That's all right. My life has been pretty screwed up, too. This is my first week selling Fords, and we're going to straighten out our lives together."

Zap—instant bonding at a soul-mate level. After proving he had a steady income, Stein's friend purchased a Mustang from the saleswoman. She had listened, demonstrated understanding and aligned her interests with his needs.

Too many times, we try to sell ideas without getting to know decision makers. This rarely works.

We must listen.
Identify. Bond.

Build RELATIONSHIPS.

John and Brendan Ready are lobstermen. And they're also relationship builders.

The brothers own Catch a Piece of Maine and use their website to grow relationships. Customers know the lobstermen's boats and their trap locations.

These clients pay $3,000 for rights to lobsters caught in a trap for one year. The brothers guarantee forty lobsters, but expect the catch to be near fifty each year.

"It's an interactive approach," says Brendan Ready. "People buy into what we're doing because they get the same excitement we have every day. They know exactly where their lobsters are coming from and who's catching them. It's really an experience."

THE READY BROTHERS SELL LOBSTERS.
THEIR CUSTOMERS BUY RELATIONSHIPS.

CATCH A PIECE OF MAINE'S
RELATIONSHIP *lessons.*

1. KNOW DECISION MAKERS AND LET THEM GET TO KNOW YOU.

2. HELP THEM UNDERSTAND AND VISUALIZE YOUR PROCESS.

3. INVOLVE THEM IN YOUR DAY-TO-DAY ACTIVITIES.

4. PROMISE WHAT YOU CAN DELIVER—AND THEN DELIVER.

5. MAKE THE RELATIONSHIP FUN AND REWARDING.

Operators
ARE STANDING BY.

The home-shopping company QVC creates thousands of relationships to sell truckloads of vegetable choppers, costume jewelry and personal electronics.

The firm builds relationships by building trust. When its exercise guru says a Pilates machine works, customers trust her opinion. And when QVC's electronics wizard gushes over a digital camera, calls pour in.

QVC uses the Internet to listen. For example, iQVC hosts chat sessions before the day's featured product is introduced on TV. Customers share views, and QVC spokespeople use their feedback to polish on-air pitches.

QVC shows appreciation to its customers by including them in product reviews, providing special offers and sending lots of thank-you messages.

QVC'S RELATIONSHIP
lessons.

1. BE HONEST ABOUT YOUR IDEAS AND CAPABILITIES.

2. EXHIBIT PASSION AND ENTHUSIASM.

3. MEET COMMITMENTS. SAY WHAT YOU'LL DO AND DO IT.

4. USE EVERY AVAILABLE TOOL TO NURTURE RELATIONSHIPS—MEETINGS, NOTES, E-MAIL, WEBSITES, ONLINE CONFERENCES, PHONE CALLS AND MORE.

5. LISTEN TO IDEAS, OBJECTIONS AND SUGGESTIONS.

6. LET DECISION MAKERS KNOW YOU VALUE RELATIONSHIPS BY APPLYING THEIR FEEDBACK AND SHOWING APPRECIATION.

SATURDAY
night live.

What does your decision maker do on a Saturday night? In other words, what do you know about his likes, dislikes, habits and lifestyle? The more you know, the better you'll connect your ideas with his wants and needs.

WORK ON YOUR relationships.

Determine actions you can take in coming months to strengthen relationships with decision makers.

DECISION MAKER:

Action Step	Start Date
1.	
2.	
3.	

DECISION MAKER:

Action Step	Start Date
1.	
2.	
3.	

DECISION MAKER:

Action Step	Start Date
1.	
2.	
3.	

emotional NEADS.

Most people seek levels of appreciation, affiliation, autonomy and authority.
Use these four touchpoints to turn emotional needs into selling opportunities.

APPRECIATION
Decision maker needs to:
- · receive recognition for his contributions
- · perceive respect for his knowledge
- · collect gratitude for his generosity and cooperation

AFFILIATION
Decision maker needs to:
- · have an emotional connection
- · feel you want to help her succeed
- · envision the team working together

AUTONOMY
Decision maker needs to:
- · know she can think, speak and act freely
- · feel your idea won't affect his independence
- · sense he'll be able to contribute 100 percent

AUTHORITY
Decision maker needs to:
- · stay in charge and in control
- · know you're accountable for your ideas and actions
- · understand you'll get things done as agreed

"IF THEY FEEL THEY *birthed it,* THEY CAN'T *kill it.*"

This advice was given to David Schimmel, And Partners creative director, early in his career at a Miami ad agency.

"The agency owner encouraged us to remove our egos from presentations and let clients take credit for ideas," says Schimmel. "His philosophy was to do everything possible to enable clients to take ownership of the process.

"I've used his advice at And Partners. We allow for client feedback at all stages. This ensures client participation and buy-in. Waiting to have the big reveal of an idea at the end of an eight-week process never gives us a positive outcome.

"If you truly collaborate with your client, there's a good chance you'll sell your strongest ideas without having them watered down."

Collaborate

WITH CLIENTS.

Many IdeaSellers build buy-in by collaborating with clients during ideation.

"When I used to go into presentations saying 'I have an idea,' I would make it too personal and precious," says Trish Berrong, creative director at Hallmark Cards. "Going into a presentation with the spark of something—and letting the group contribute to the energy of the idea and make it their own—is almost always more successful for us."

Because of this success, Berrong says her team often holds work sessions with clients rather than a series of formal presentations.

"This doesn't mean I'm not prepared to defend great ideas," she says, "or that I don't recognize the difference between collaborating and 'committeeing' the life out an idea.

"Group mind—wiring brains together and elevating thoughts—and group think—chaining brains together and sinking to the lowest point—are two very different processes."

INVOLVE
DECISION MAKERS.

Before generating ideas for your next project, anticipate steps you'll
be taking from start to finish. Decide how to involve decision makers
in any or all steps.

PROJECT:

STEP:
DECISION MAKER INVOLVEMENT:

STEP:
DECISION MAKER INVOLVEMENT:

STEP:
DECISION MAKER INVOLVEMENT:

ONE BRICK
at a time.

Hallmark's Trish Berrong performs with an improv comedy group during her off hours and finds the experience helps when collaborating with clients.

"With improv, you're working with other performers to quickly come up with ideas," she says, "and the process almost always results in something greater than any one person could conceive alone.

"And there's a sense of play in the work, which immediately lowers defenses and puts everybody on the same side.

"It's great when client meetings and presentations are like that. When you leave the room, you have The Idea—and everyone owns it, everyone champions it. It's bigger than any one person—it belongs to the group.

"AT MY BEST, I REMEMBER I'M NOT BUILDING THE WALL— I'M BRINGING A BRICK."

HITCH YOUR IDEA
to a star.

Our team wanted to sell high-end stationery and home desk items using a magalog—a combination of a magazine and direct-mail catalog—with editorial content as well as products.

To fund this high-end project, we had to convince decision makers of its value, so we began by familiarizing them with the magalog genre.

We created a glide path for acceptance by hitching our ideas to stars. Before revealing our prototypes, we showed decision makers samples of successful magalogs, like those from Patagonia and Neiman Marcus.

We walked decision makers through the catalogs, discussing product positioning, editorial approaches and marketing techniques. We shared sales figures garnered from industry publications and our extrapolations.

These preliminary showings eased the eventual selling of our ideas. When we presented prototypes in the following weeks, decision makers were already at the "understand" and even "accept" positions on the Buyer's Bench (see page 12).

Facing the tough sell of an unfamiliar idea?

FIND SUCCESS STORIES WITH APPROACHES SIMILAR TO YOUR CONCEPT, WHETHER IN THE SAME INDUSTRY OR DISTANT FIELDS.

Use these to inform and guide decision makers.

Shine YOUR OWN STARS.

You can often sell an idea by hitching it to stars from other industries, as discussed on the previous page. Or perhaps a lucky star from your own past can help sell the new idea.

That's how Stefan Mumaw of Reign Agency pitched unfamiliar TV spots to a retail client. The concept revolved around a funny character that originally seemed far outside the client's comfort level.

"They were leaning toward a more familiar Nike-type spot," Mumaw says, "something displaying the passion and athleticism of tennis players."

To help overcome resistance to something less familiar, Mumaw pulled stars from the agency's past campaigns. "We showed examples of ads that had stretched other clients in new directions," he says. "And when we discussed the financial success of those creative leaps, the decision makers agreed to do the spots. Our track record made the difference."

HOW'S THEIR DAY

looking?

Before booking a meeting or presentation, find out what's going on in your decision maker's world. Get to know her assistant. Talk to her co-workers.

If you're making an appointment directly, say something like: "Maria, I'm excited about this idea, so I want to catch you when you're not overbooked—is next Wednesday a relatively calm day for you?"

Of course, last-minute crises still happen. You arrive at the appointed time, all sunshine and peaches, and there's frost in the air. One look at the client's face says you should be wearing body armor.

Ask to reschedule. Say to the edgy client: "I'm not psychic, but it's pretty clear this isn't the best moment to be taking up your time. Why don't I come back in a day or two?"

The client will usually agree—probably looking relieved, maybe managing a weak smile. When you do return, you'll receive extra consideration.

PAY ATTENTION TO TIMING. IDEAS ARE TOO IMPORTANT TO BLOW ON BAD DAYS.

Don't be
A TIME BANDIT.

"Got a minute?"

There's a loaded question. You may indeed have a minute, but not want to spend it with the person asking. And you can bet the discussion would take longer than sixty seconds.

Equally criminal is the tired sales technique of asking for "just five minutes to tell you about an idea," knowing even a rapid-fire overview will take half an hour.

To be considered credible, be considerate of people's time. Provide honest estimates of how long your presentation will take. Be on time. Start on time. Finish on time.

Of course, there'll be situations where the decision maker will knock you off schedule with windy comments or constant questions. Don't cut him off—just let him know you're aware of the clock: "Steve, I'm delighted you're interested enough in this idea to ask questions, and I'm eager to answer them—but I also want to respect your time. Are you OK with giving me an extra fifteen minutes?"

PEOPLE TREASURE THEIR TIME. DON'T STEAL IT.

"If you want someone to think you're selfish, just ask for a minute of their time and then waste it or use it for your own ends."

—Seth Godin

"Is now a good time?"

A certain designer would always ask that question before entering my office to show an idea—even when he had an appointment.

It's no coincidence Greg had a higher idea approval ratio than others on my team.

Sure, Greg was highly talented, but my acceptance of his ideas owed much to the power of his asking, "Is now a good time for me to show you an idea?"

Because he showed respect for my time, I would usually sit back and wave him in. But if I was deep in thought or scrambling to meet a deadline, I'd suggest a better time.

Either way, Greg won. If I said OK, he had my eyes and ears. And if I said no, he avoided having to pitch to a distracted, impatient guy across the table.

Psychological genius, that Greg.

Who DECIDES?

Maybe your decision maker says, "I'm all for your idea—now let me see if Shirley approves, and I'll get back with you."

Uh oh. He went to Shirley with your last idea and came back empty-handed. How do you make sure he doesn't blow this deal?

1. ASK TO BE IN ON THE MEETING. Say: "I know this idea inside and out. What if I joined in to answer questions or help make the pitch?"

2. IF HE LETS YOU PARTICIPATE, PREPARE YOURSELF. Learn everything you can about the top decision maker. Ask your boss for hints—dos and don'ts, hot buttons, pet peeves. Don't assume—make sure your decision maker clarifies what he expects from you. Be a team player. Not "me," but "we." Not "I," but "us."

3. IF HE DOESN'T LET YOU PARTICIPATE, PREPARE HIM. Provide props, handouts and visuals fitting his style. Offer cheat sheets, insight cards and prototypes. If you can walk him through a rehearsal, do so. Ask what else he needs to sell your idea. Ask again. And again.

After all, the future of your idea is in his hands.

"A great presentation will give the client all the tools he or she needs to then turn around and sell the idea internally."

—Sally Hogshead, AUTHOR AND COPYWRITER

Pad *and* pen.

I love it when doctors take notes while I'm talking. And auto service managers. Real estate agents. Even dog sitters.

They're listening to what I'm saying. They care. My words are important enough to write down.

Decision makers also feel better if you're taking notes. You're acknowledging the value of their viewpoints. You're showing interest and concern.

But those are side effects. The main reason for taking notes is to capture key points. You'll collect a treasure chest of insights for refining concepts and building relationships.

Open a notebook when you're in front of decision makers.

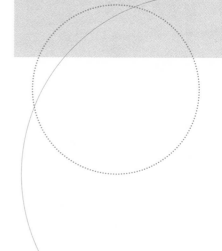

When they talk, you write.

NOTES ON
note-taking.

1. WRITE NOTES, NOT NOVELS.
Jot down key words, not complete sentences—just enough to remind you of suggestions, concerns and action steps. Review notes as soon as you return to your desk, and fill in the blanks.

2. REMEMBER EYE CONTACT.
Writing without looking takes practice, but it's worth mastering. Otherwise, glance down to make fast notes, but quickly reestablish eye contact. Nobody enjoys talking to the top of a tilted head.

3. ID THE PAGES.
Write the meeting date or a key word in the top right corner of each filled page in your notebook. When you're trying to find info later, you can easily thumb through the pages.

2

Begin by *boosting* YOUR BELIEVABILITY.

"To be persuasive we must be believable; to be believable we must be credible; to be credible we must be truthful."

—Edward R. Murrow, JOURNALIST

Ethos, *pathos,* LOGOS.

According to Aristotle's Rhetorical Triangle, the three elements of persuasion are ethos, pathos and logos.

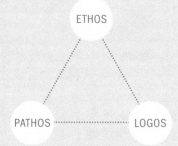

ETHOS—ethics, credibility, character of the presenter

PATHOS—passion, emotion, the presenter's connection with the audience

LOGOS—logic, reasoning, data to support the presenter's topic

ARISTOTLE,
the IdeaSeller.

When persuading people to buy ideas, Aristotle's triad lights the road to success.

> *Selling is all about what's going on in the hearts and minds of decision makers.*

ETHOS: Can I trust this presenter? Can I believe her? Does she know the value of her idea? Does she understand my wants and needs? Does she have the solution to my problem?

PATHOS: Does the presenter understand me? Is he passionate about his idea and what it can do for me? Does he know what makes me happy? What makes me sad and fearful? Do we have a connection, a chemistry, a bond?

LOGOS: Is this presenter reasonable? Does she make sense? Does she understand my objectives? Does she realize I won't approve her idea unless I feel it benefits me?

Build BELIEVABILITY.

We tune out people we don't believe—be they managers or mechanics, professors or politicians, relatives or researchers.

Sometimes these folks lose credibility because they don't seem to know what they're talking about. Other times they come across as insincere. And other times they look lifeless or have dirty nails.

THE THREE COMPONENTS
OF CREDIBILITY ARE:

COMPETENCE: knowledge, skill, experience

TRUSTWORTHINESS: honesty, sincerity, integrity

ATTRACTION: appearance, energy, confidence

Credibility is the believability of a person as judged by another person. And selling ideas calls for heaping helpings of credibility with decision makers.

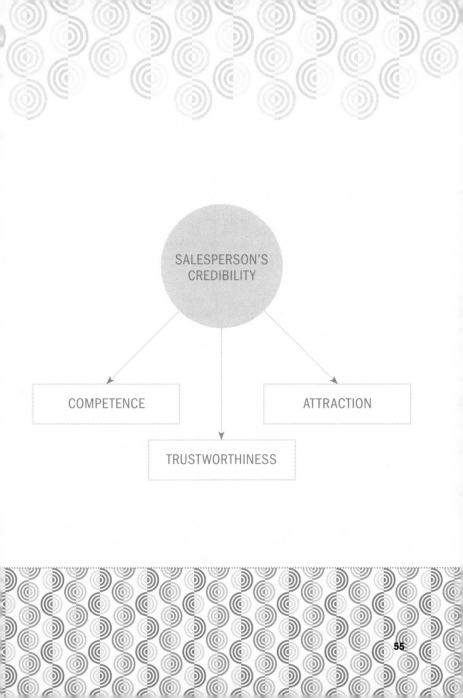

SALESPERSON'S
CREDIBILITY

COMPETENCE

ATTRACTION

TRUSTWORTHINESS

NO CREDIBILITY,
no champagne.

If a presenter lacks credibility, there'll be no corks popping after the pitch. Credibility is the sine qua non of selling ideas.

What's really happening in decision makers' minds when they sense an absence of credibility? They're probably thinking:

"He doesn't know what he's talking about."

The decision maker perceives a lack of competence. The presenter comes across as unskilled or unprofessional.

"I don't believe a word she says."

The decision maker finds the person lacking trustworthiness. She's perceived as insincere, dishonest or off-base. Or totally self-focused, with little regard for the decision maker's needs and interests.

"Borrrrring."

The decision maker is stifling yawns, or is turned off by the presenter's appearance or demeanor. He's perceived as lacking attraction—dull, inexpressive or unappealing.

CREDIBILITY = COMPETENCE + TRUSTWORTHINESS + ATTRACTION

COMING ACROSS
as competent?

"A human being should be able to change a diaper, plan an invasion, butcher a hog, conn a ship, design a building, write a sonnet, balance accounts, build a wall, set a bone, comfort the dying, take orders, give orders, cooperate, act alone, solve equations, analyze a new problem, pitch manure, program a computer, cook a tasty meal, fight efficiently, die gallantly."

—Robert Heinlein, TIME ENOUGH FOR LOVE

Whoa—few of us would rank high on the competence scale with metrics put forth by one of Heinlein's characters.

But we get his point. To be perceived as competent, we have to register as resourceful. Thinking must be deep and wide. We can't appear shallow, narrow or shortsighted.

In addition to exhibiting expertise in his specialty, an IdeaSeller must show savoir faire about the world, as well as an understanding of his decision maker's world—her likes, dislikes, responsibilities, audiences, wants and needs.

The renowned architect Renzo Piano exudes competence. When presenting his ideas for expanding Manhattan's Morgan Library, Piano demonstrated not only his vast knowledge of architecture, but also his understanding of American culture, industrial values, diverse building materials—and how piazzas function in Italy's Renaissance villages.

AS YOU
probably KNOW...

You can sometimes underscore credibility with positive presumptions, such as:

"As you probably know..."

"As you're aware..."

"As you understand..."

These lead-ins ease people into accepting your statements. Or cause them to pretend they know something they actually don't. You'll rarely have someone jump in to say, "No, I'm so stupid I don't know the first thing about that."

Positive presumptions aren't to deceive or mislead, but rather to help convey truths in a convincing, diplomatic way.

Such statements also allow face-saving. For example, if you've uncovered a fact about the decision maker's customers that he should know but likely doesn't, you might say: "As I'm sure already you know, Marcus, 30 percent of customers..."

USE POSITIVE PRESUMPTIONS SPARINGLY, BUT EMPLOY THEM. THEY INDUCE ACCEPTANCE AND CREDIBILITY.

"You can trust me."

You've heard that line, right? And did you trust the person?

Unlikely. When people say to us "I'm honest" or "I'm trustworthy," our skepticism rises. The more a person professes his honesty, the less we tend to believe him. Instead, we perceive trustworthiness through a person's speech, behavior, actions and background.

How do you demonstrate your trustworthiness to decision makers?

Fortunately, trust is a more common reflex than skepticism. Our society depends on trust, whether it's loaning books, assuming drivers will stop for red lights or accepting websites' rules without reading fine print.

"The default is trust until there's a reason not to," says Robyn Dawes, a psychologist at Carnegie Mellon University.

IN OTHER WORDS, YOU MIGHT BE GRANTED A LEVEL OF TRUST THE FIRST TIME YOU MEET WITH DECISION MAKERS. YOURS TO LOSE—OR GROW.

TRUST-BUILDING

INGREDIENTS.

1. Background: Supply recommendations, testimonials and success stories—but not from a boastful or pompous place. Use them sparingly and humbly.

2. Track record: Meet commitments, large and small—deadlines, budgets, phone calls and e-mails. Say what you'll do, do what you say.

3. Nonverbal communications: We constantly signal trustworthiness with body language and eye contact. Learn how nonverbal behavior affects perceptions. (See page 120 for examples.) Watch for and correct any negative signals when rehearsing pitches.

"When the eyes say one thing, and the tongue another, a practiced man relies on the language of the first."

—Ralph Waldo Emerson

Looking good.

Credibility's third component is attraction—appearance, energy and confidence.

Let's quickly get personal appearance out of the way, particularly when it comes to dress. Many variables apply to clothing, so it's impossible to give one-size-fits-all pointers. What's appropriate depends on the industry, workplace, region, season, age, sex, nationality and more.

Wear what works. You're making the pitch to sell your idea. Dress to make the sale. Sometimes that means dressing up, other times dressing down. Don't dress to make statements about anything other than the sale. Wear what works.

As for other areas of personal appearance—hairstyle, hygiene and halitosis—peg a friend or family member and ask for straight talk. Take it with a smile. Say thank you. Adjust accordingly.

No need to look like a Vogue or GQ model when selling ideas, but make your mama proud. After all, nobody's ever had an idea rejected because he or she looked too good.

A showman
SUITS UP.

Designer Marc English is a familiar face on the lecture circuit. He's known for his on-stage costumes, such as African turbans, Scottish kilts and mariachi outfits.

The morning after one of English's wild and upbeat lectures, someone asked if he would wear the same outfit to a client meeting as the one he wore on stage the previous night.

"Of course not," English told the person. "You got the rock-and-roll show last night. There's theater, and there's the real world."

For idea pitches, English dresses for the client. "I'll wear suit and tie if I think the clients will be dressed that way," he says, "and I always try to wear a suit as good as or better than the client's."

If the meeting is at his own studio, English puts suits aside in the name of authenticity. "The clients would take one look around the studio and realize I was over-dressed," he says. "So I may wear jeans and T-shirt or jacket and slacks, depending on the client."

CONVEY
CONFIDENCE.

Think of your favorite speaker. Maybe a politician or technology guru. Architect or designer. Author or actor. Lawyer or doctor. Teacher or spiritual leader. Executive or scientist. Family member or friend.

I'll bet he or she exudes confidence. Confidence in herself. Confidence in her ideas.

So how do you display confidence?

1. BE SOLD YOURSELF. Believe in yourself and your ideas. It shows.

2. EXHIBIT ENERGY. No need to leap onto tables or shake tambourines, but radiate robustness. If you look tired, your ideas look tired.

3. STAND STRAIGHT. Our parents nagged about this, and for good reason. Posture influences perceived confidence. Stand and sit straight, but relaxed—stiffness is seen as nervousness.

4. GESTURE NATURALLY. Use your hands when you talk. But don't be mechanical or overly forceful. And watch for gestures conveying nervousness, such as playing with pens or constantly moving your legs. Have friends point out your personal tics, or watch yourself on video.

5. FACE UP. Know what you're communicating with facial expressions. A friend was pitching an idea when his boss stopped him. "Are you excited about this idea?" asked the boss. "Sure," said my friend. "Then for God's sake, tell your face," said the boss.

SMALL details.

Nike once asked Tiger Woods to test its prototypes of a new driver. He hit with three of the sample clubs and said he liked the lighter one.

The clubs all weigh exactly the same, Nike's designer told Woods. No, this one is lighter, he replied.

They placed the drivers on a scale and discovered that Woods was right—the club he preferred weighed two grams less than the others. Two grams—the weight of a couple of paper clips.

To generate confidence and be perceived as an expert, master even the smallest details of your idea.

SPOT-CHECK *your credibility.*

COMPETENT

Am I perceived as someone who can handle the project?

Do I know my specialty—and also have broader knowledge and experience?

TRUSTWORTHY

Do people believe what I say?

Do I have a track record of meeting commitments?

ATTRACTIVE

Does my appearance tend to attract or repel people?

Do I project positive energy and confidence?

3

LEARN BY ASKING *all the right* QUESTIONS.

"The art and science of asking questions
is the source of all knowledge."

—Thomas Berger, NOVELIST

BE *curious.*

Highly creative people are highly curious people.

"One of the most important keys to acting is curiosity," Meryl Streep told *The New York Times*. "I am curious to the point of being nosy. What that means is you want to devour lives. You're eager to put on their shoes and wear their clothes and have them become a part of you."

Curiosity inspires creativity by taking us into the minds of our audiences. We see through different eyes.

And curiosity makes us stronger IdeaSellers.

If we're curious about decision makers—if we try to walk in their shoes—we'll better understand how they think and act. We'll learn how they make decisions.

Be curious about employees, shareholders, customers, competitors. Be curious about top lines and bottom lines. Be curious about successes and failures.

Be curious to the point of being nosy.

Ask questions.

Questions are secret weapons of selling. Keys to the kingdom. Code breakers. Especially when you start probing early and continue until the final OK.

QUESTIONS HELP YOU GATHER INSIGHTS. DISCOVER NEEDS. ANALYZE OBJECTIVES. DIG INTO OBJECTIONS. OVERCOME OBSTACLES. UNDERSTAND THE DECISION MAKER'S THOUGHTS, FEELINGS AND ATTITUDES.

"You get lots of information if you just ask the right questions," says Loop9 Marketing's Cathy Austin. "Most folks enjoy telling you about what they know."

And once they've told you about their business, you can use their words in your presentation. "Talking their talk builds instant credibility," Austin says, "and consequently helps clients become much more receptive to ideas."

ASKING *enough* QUESTIONS?

RECALL AN IDEA THAT ENDED IN REJECTION. LIST QUESTIONS YOU ASKED YOUR DECISION MAKER BEFORE AND DURING THE PRESENTATION:

WHAT ADDITIONAL QUESTIONS SHOULD YOU HAVE ASKED?

Make a copy of this page. Review it when you're preparing to present your next idea.

Two types
OF QUESTIONS.

According to marketing expert Seth Godin, there are
two kinds of questions:

1. QUESTIONS TO OBTAIN MORE INFORMATION.

2. QUESTIONS TO DEMONSTRATE HOW MUCH
YOU KNOW, OR TO ILLUSTRATE YOUR POSITION
ON AN ISSUE.

"There's room for both types of questions," he says,
"particularly in a team preparing for a pitch.

"Don't confuse them. I like to be sure that there's time
for the first type, then, once everyone acknowledges
that they know what's on the table, open it up for the
second, more debate-oriented type of question."

Dig.

Don't stop with surface questions. Dig down so decision makers go deeper. That's when you'll discover insights.

"How did the sales force let you down?"

"What are your personal goals for recruiting?"

"What obstacles stand in the way of a record year?"

"What level of attendance would you consider a huge success?"

"Can you give me a picture of what a successful event would look like?"

Of course, never begin a meeting with questions like these. And avoid streams of rapid-fire inquiries that make you sound like a prosecuting attorney.

DIG DOWN. BUT USE A SPADE, NOT A BULLDOZER.

OPEN-ENDED
QUESTIONS.

Open-ended questions solicit thoughtful replies rather than one-word responses. So you'll bag more insights.

Open-ended questions usually begin with words like "how" and "why." Or they may be statements rather than questions, opening with phrases such as "walk me through..." or "tell me about..."

"How does this project compare to similar ones you've seen in the past?"

"Why do you think shareholders haven't responded to mailers?"

"What's the normal approval process for this type of project?"

"Walk me through a day in the life of one of your sales managers."

"Tell me what it feels like to go out and talk with employees about this."

To avoid being overbearing, balance open-ended questions with closed-ended ones that allow short responses.

OPEN-ENDED *practice.*

EXERCISE 1:

Imagine you're across the table from your favorite actor, author or designer.
List five open-ended questions you would ask.

1.
2.
3.
4.
5.

EXERCISE 2:

Construct three open-ended questions to ask your boss or another decision maker
the next time you're together. Think of questions to open discussions about his or
her likes, dislikes, wants and needs.

1.
2.
3.

EXERCISE 3:

For the next week, practice asking open-ended questions during conversations with
friends, family and co-workers. Balance these with closed-ended questions.

"How come"
QUESTIONS.

Sometimes questions need to be as simple as those of kids. I call these "how come" questions. Spend time around a child, and you'll get an earful:

"How come there's no number lower than zero?"

"How come I can blow my nose but not my ears?"

"How come teddy bears don't grow up to become grizzly bears?"

No pretense. No need to impress. Just a need to know.

There are times we need to ask "how come" questions, perhaps with an adult twist. Something like:

"Anita, we noticed a declining trend in customers using the company's mainte-nance service. How come?"

"How come" questions also help when you need to ask sensitive questions with a touch of naiveté:

"Craig, whenever I mention this project to your managers, they seem a bit defen-sive or uptight—how come?"

"HOW COME" QUESTIONS SHOULD NOT REPLACE RESEARCH. BUT USE THEM WHEN YOU WANT A STRAIGHT ANSWER TO A STRAIGHT QUESTION. LIKE A KID.

Question
YOUR QUESTIONING.

1. ARE YOUR QUESTIONS TOO AGGRESSIVE?

Are you coming on too strong? Are your questions abrasive or accusatory? People react to the way questions are asked as much as to what's actually asked. Practice with friends or co-workers, and encourage them to judge your delivery.

2. ARE YOU LISTENING TO ANSWERS?

Sometimes we're so busy preparing to ask our next question that we don't listen to the answer being given. Concentrate on what's being said.

3. ARE YOU TAKING NOTES?

Write down key points and details. Ask for clarification and elaboration.

4. ARE YOU ACKNOWLEDGING ANSWERS?

Don't keep moving down a list of questions without acknowledging answers. Take a moment to simply say "thank you." And if the answer is insightful, make comments like "that makes things clearer" or "that really helps." People like sincere praise and feedback.

5. ARE YOU PAUSING BEFORE THE NEXT QUESTION?

After your decision maker answers, nod—but also pause before commenting or asking your next question. She'll often add another comment—and it's usually just the information you need. And even if she's done, the short break will give her time to recharge before the next question.

LAST QUESTION
to ask.

Whether I'm discussing an idea or interviewing for my writings, I almost always wrap up with this:

> *"What other questions should I be asking you?"*

I then break eye contact, usually glancing up and into the distance—as if I'm also trying to think of more questions. I sit quietly.

This usually brings about more insights. Sometimes the person says, "Well, you might ask how I really feel about..." or "You might want to know why we've always been reluctant to try projects like this..."

Other times the person launches into added commentary, such as "When we were talking a few minutes ago, I thought about a time when..." or "One issue we probably need to explore is..."

Our questions will never uncover everything. Give the decision maker a chance to help. End with "What other questions should I be asking you?"

4

Find out
WHAT CLIENTS WANT
by listening.

"You seldom listen to me, and when you do
you don't hear, and when you do hear you hear
wrong, and even when you hear right you
change it so fast that it's never the same."

—Marjorie Kellogg, AUTHOR
   AND SCREENWRITER

Listen up.

"I encourage everyone on our team to be good listeners," says David Schimmel of And Partners. "We present the work, then sit back and listen to feedback. Our clients know their business and can help make the ideas stronger."

Jeff Long of Digital Kitchen agrees. "Really listen to what people are saying," he says. "Understand the room."

Listen to what decision makers are telling you. Listen closely. Try not to think about what you're going to say next.

Relax and simply listen.

"Big egos have little ears."
—Dr. Robert Schuller, MINISTER AND AUTHOR

Practice LISTENING.

We're taught to talk. And to write. But we're never taught to listen.
Train yourself to be a better listener. Try these exercises:

LISTENING EXERCISE 1:

Sit alone in a public place—maybe a park, airport, coffee shop or restaurant. Relax.
Use your ears as directional microphones to pick up sounds and conversations.
Focus on what you're hearing.

LISTENING EXERCISE 2:

During conversations, deliberately concentrate on listening. Notice when you're
tuning out. Catch yourself interrupting or thinking about what you're going to say next.
Work on staying focused and in the moment.

LISTENING EXERCISE 3:

Persuade a friend or family member to let you ask five questions. Have in mind the
first question you'll ask—but only the first question. Carefully listen to the response,
pause, and then ask a second question building on the first answer. Continue until
you've asked five questions.

REPEAT THIS EXERCISE WITH FIVE PEOPLE. NOTICE IMPROVEMENTS IN YOUR
LISTENING AND QUESTIONING SKILLS.

"The best salespeople are great listeners. That's how you find out what the buyer wants."

—Spencer Johnson, AUTHOR

"I think the one lesson I have learned is there is no substitute for paying attention."

—Diane Sawyer, TV ANCHOR

"Nothing I say this day will teach me anything. So if I'm going to learn, I must do it by listening."

—Larry King, TV INTERVIEWER

Poor LISTENING HABITS.

1. *Finishing the speaker's sentences.*
2. *Thinking about what to ask or say next.*
3. *Yielding to distractions.*
4. *Glancing at PDA, cell phone and printed materials.*
5. *Interrupting the speaker.*
6. *Looking around the room.*
7. *Tuning out.*

MAKE EYE CONTACT
while listening.

Maintain eye contact when listening, not just when talking. By doing this, you're showing interest, building bonds, establishing trust. Of course, other listening skills should accompany eye contact, such as nodding and offering feedback.

But when someone across the table talks nonstop for several minutes, give eye contact a break. Your stare can be off-putting and distracting.

When you break eye contact, be careful not to scan the room or look over the talker's shoulder. That's a sure way to irritate the person and diminish trust.

Having a notepad helps. Glance down and jot a word or two. This breaks eye contact—and lets the listener know her words are valuable enough to record.

MAKE EYE CONTACT
while talking.

You're on 7th Avenue in Manhattan, listening as a street vendor tells about the watches on his table. You don't need a watch, so why are you giving him your time?

Eye contact. He's locked eyes with you throughout his spiel. And it works. You want to trust this guy. And in a New York minute, you walk away with a watch.

"An important behavior for increasing credibility is to maintain eye contact while communicating," says James P.T. Fatt, a lecturer at Singapore's Nanyang Technological University. "Shifting eyes, looking down at notes and blinking excessively have been shown to lower credibility."

When you're presenting one-on-one, focus on eye contact, especially when making key points. But don't intensely stare—that gets a bit creepy. Break contact for a few seconds by looking up or to the side, as if pondering or remembering something.

When talking to a group, make eye contact with one person at a time. Stay with the person for a sentence or two, then move to the next person. That way, you'll include everyone and build trust.

know
THE CULTURE.

These comments about eye contact apply in Western societies. In certain regions of the world, such as east Asia, direct eye contact with a boss or older person may signal aggressiveness, rudeness or disrespect.

THREE DAYS to better eye contact.

DAY 1:

Establish eye contact with people whose paths you cross during the day—co-workers, shopkeepers, cashiers, family members and others.

Pay attention to reactions. Do they return the contact or look away? Do they smile or seem uncomfortable? Are they engaged or distant? Notice your own reactions. At the end of the day, write about your discoveries.

DAY 2:

Make eye contact within a group—at team meetings, family gatherings, lunch tables. While you're talking, look at each person for a sentence or two, then move to the next person. Observe reactions. Do they return eye contact or glance away? Once you've establish contact, does the person seem more interested? Does he or she nod in agreement? Notice if others in the group make eye contact when they're talking. At day's end, write about your experiences.

DAY 3:

Throughout the day, establish eye contact when listening to people. Practice locking in, then glancing away. Check your level of comfort with this process. Notice the reactions of the talkers. Write about these episodes.

Eye exam.

QUESTION: You're presenting an idea to your decision maker. You've learned about the value of eye contact, so you're locked in. She interrupts to ask an important question. You need a second to think of a meaningful answer. Do you maintain contact or glance away?

ANSWER: Definitely look away—either upward or to the side. British researchers found subjects correctly answered more than 70 percent of questions when they looked away before answering. When subjects held eye contact while thinking, they correctly answered only 50 percent of questions.

"Human faces are very stimulating and take mental processing," says Dr. Gwyneth Doherty-Sneddon, a psychologist at the University of Stirling. *"When we are trying to process something that's mentally demanding, it's unhelpful to look at faces."*

5

SUCCESS =
OPPORTUNITY
+ PREPARATION

"Success always comes when preparation
meets opportunity."

—Henry Hartman, ARTIST AND DESIGNER

PREPARE.

Are you preparing for presentations? Or are you winging it?

Don't be a wing nut. Instead, follow the lead of award-winning actors who rehearse and prepare.

Take, for example, Philip Seymour Hoffman, one of the best character actors of our time. Although he makes it look easy, Hoffman works hard, obsessively preparing for every role.

For his Oscar-winning performance in *Capote*, he spent four months working on his character. "Playing Capote took a lot of concentration," says Hoffman. "I read and listened to his voice and watched videos of him on TV... I was speaking in a voice that my vocal cords did not want to do. I had to stay in character all day."

Athletes also know preparation's power. Michael Jordan invested so much of himself into preparation that every Bulls practice felt like the last game of the NBA finals.

"Nothing replaces practice, even if you're a natural-born salesperson," says Don McNeill, president of Digital Kitchen.

"THERE'S A DIFFERENCE BETWEEN KNOWING WHAT YOU'VE CREATED AND KNOWING HOW TO SELL IT."

PREPARE
with *patience*.

Julie Taymor, director of the play *The Lion King* and films such as *Frida* and *Across the Universe*, tells of traveling through Indonesia as a young woman to study puppetry and mask-making.

In one village, she looked on as a mask-maker prepared for his day's work. The master craftsman slowly unrolled a worn leather pouch, carefully removed his tools and gently placed them on his worktable.

His simple act became an indelible example for Taymor, forever reminding her that true craftsmanship demands patience and exactness.

In the mad rush to get ideas into action, it's tempting to throw presentations together willy-nilly. We work overtime to develop glorious ideas, then shortcut the process of selling them.

Step back. Craft the pitch. Your idea's worth it.

Don't jump the gun.

Like runners at starter blocks, we sometimes push off too quickly to pitch ideas. Hopped up on adrenaline, we rush for approvals—often before we or our decision makers are ready.

Don't disqualify ideas by jumping the gun. Get ready, get set, then go.

BEFORE YOU PITCH,

MASTER THE CLIMB.

Preparing for his first Tour de France, Lance Armstrong biked up a body-breaking mountain. Because of wind, snow and sleet, it took him four hours to reach the top.

But when the follow car tried to pick up Armstrong at the summit, he refused, saying he would have to do it all over again.

"I did it," he told his trainer, "but I don't know how I did it. I don't yet understand the climb."

Armstrong rode his bike back down the mountain, then worked his way back up.

Only then did he feel he had mastered the climb.

Are you mastering presentations before making pitches?

DELIBERATE
practice.

Star athletes, artists and business people reach the top because of natural abilities, right?

Wrong. Top achievers in any field devote thousands of hours to what researchers call "deliberate practice."

Deliberate practice is designed to:

- push beyond existing competence
- involve high repetition
- provide feedback

Shooting hoops isn't deliberate practice. Shooting from one spot two hundred times, measuring results and making adjustments—every day for hours each day—is deliberate practice. That's how Michael Jordan became the world's best basketball player.

As kids, Venus and Serena Williams didn't just play a few games of tennis once or twice a week. They spent hours every day whacking 550 tennis balls on a cracked asphalt court and getting their father's feedback.

Bill Gates started programming computers when he was eight years old. Warren Buffett has spent thousands of hours studying financial statements of hundreds of companies.

PRACTICE—DELIBERATE PRACTICE— REALLY DOES MAKE PERFECT.

"If I don't practice for a day, I know it. If I don't practice for two days, my wife knows it. If I don't practice for three days, the world knows it."

—Vladimir Horowitz, PIANIST

Practice YOUR PITCH.

To perfect your pitch, try deliberate practice.

Stretch yourself.

Make a list of three presentation skills you want to improve.

1.
2.
3.

During the next three months, practice with determination on one skill at a time.

Gather feedback.

Watch yourself present in a mirror. Video your practices and review footage. Listen to audio captures of practices and critique yourself. Have friends, family and co-workers watch you practice. Ask for honest feedback.

Repeat, repeat, repeat.

Deliberate practice demands high repetition. Practice the same skill again and again—each time drawing feedback and making adjustments.

KEEP PRACTICING.
KEEP GATHERING FEEDBACK.
KEEP STRETCHING.

"If you're not practicing, somebody else is somewhere, and he'll
be ready to take your job."

—Brooks Robinson,
BASEBALL STAR

"Any idea-selling skills I have were developed
with time and work. And then more time. And
then more work. I was never convinced I was
the smartest guy in the room. So I always had to
work harder."

—Brian Collins, FOUNDER AND
CHIEF CREATIVE OFFICER OF COLLINS:

FORCEFUL,
but friendly.

The poet James Dickey once said he prepared 150 drafts of every poem—the first hundred were to get it perfect, and the last fifty were to make it sound spontaneous.

Dickey's approach to poetry also works for pitches.

Polish your presentation until it shines. Know it in and out. Be prepared. But once you're ready, find ways to come across as spontaneous and accessible, not canned and mechanical.

Work hard to make the pitch forceful. Then work equally hard to make it friendly.

sprezzatura.

Sprezzatura is an Italian word for the art of making something difficult look easy. Practice your pitch to perfection—then work on ways to display sprezzatura.

OBSERVE
other speakers.

LEARN PRESENTATION TECHNIQUES BY WATCHING SPEAKERS YOU ADMIRE—PROFESSORS, POLITICIANS, MINISTERS, TV PERSONALITIES, CONFERENCE PRESENTERS.

The TED Conference website is an excellent place to watch bright people present bright ideas.

The TED Conference began in 1984 as a gathering for idea people in technology, entertainment and design. Over the years, its scope has broadened. TED now brings together many of the world's most creative thinkers, asking them to give the talk of their lives in eighteen minutes.

TED makes hundreds of these energetic and information-loaded talks available at www.ted.com.

"TED speakers blaze onto the stage like stand-up comics, hell-bent on room domination. Some consult notes and stay close by their audiovisual equipment—PowerPoint is used for emphasis, but it never directs the talks—while others pace, spread their arms wide and take up space... What's really on display is much more right brain, and that's what I've come to be addicted to; the exposure to vigorous minds whirring as they work hard."

—Virginia Heffernan, COLUMNIST,
THE NEW YORK TIMES MAGAZINE

TED tutoring.

Spend three hours this week observing TED speakers at www.ted.com. You'll see some of the world's most creative people present their best ideas in less than twenty minutes.

1. REVIEW VARIOUS SPEAKERS. Watch and listen. Then watch without the audio. Try listening without visuals. What works? What doesn't work? Why?

2. ASSESS EACH SPEAKER'S CREDIBILITY. Measure believability. Trustworthiness. Confidence. Speaking speed. Pitch. Volume. Gestures. Posture. Energy. Nervous habits. Personal tics. Visual aids. How effective is he or she in getting the idea across? If you were the decision maker, would you accept the idea? Why or why not?

3. OVERLAY THE FOUR "C"S—CLARITY, CONTENT, CREATIVITY AND CRAFT. Determine which talks rise to excellence and why.

Take notes. Find ways to apply techniques that work to your presentations.

CREATE *situations.*

When preparing a pitch, do you see yourself as a puppet rather than puppeteer? Do you assume decision makers will pull the strings and you can only dress up, show up and hope for the best?

Take a different approach. Give yourself power. After all, you're the designer of your presentation. And as its designer, you can create situations that sway the behavior of decision makers and inspire shared visions.

"Design is powerful because it can create situations," says Dr. Richard Farson, author of *The Power of Design.* "And a situation is more determining of what people will do than personality, character, habit, genetics or any other aspect of individual makeup."

To clarify situational behavior, Dr. Farson uses the example of a round table and a rectangular table. "Seat a group of people at a rectangular table and watch how they interact," he says. "Then put those same people at a round table. Notice the immediate increase in energy, conversation and interaction."

We've all experienced effects of situations on our attitudes, thinking and energy—dark or light-filled rooms, comfortable or uncomfortable chairs, compelling or boring visuals.

Different situations lead us to act in different ways. Design your pitch's every detail—seating, lighting, visuals, materials, stories, examples—to positively influence decision makers and create shared visions.

Know the room.

Musicians check out concert halls before performances. Football players check out stadiums before games.

Chefs check kitchens before cooking. Surgeons check operating rooms before cutting. Speakers check auditoriums before speaking.

Check out the room before presenting your idea. Pay an advance visit. Study lighting and seating. Review AV equipment. Sit where you'll be sitting. Stand where you'll be standing.

VISUALIZE YOURSELF IN ACTION. MOVE AROUND. FEEL THE ROOM. GET TO KNOW IT.

You'll discover what needs improving or changing—in the room or in your pitch. And you'll arrive confident because you'll walk into a familiar space.

PRESENTATION ROOM *checklist.*

LIGHT

- ☐ Is there an ideal light level for slides or a computer screen?
- ☐ Is there an ideal light level for hand-held visuals and eye contact?
- ☐ Does lighting add or reduce energy in the room?

SOUND

- ☐ Will decision makers be able to easily hear you?
- ☐ Will you be able to easily hear decision makers?
- ☐ Are there any distracting sounds from the AC or piped-in music?
- ☐ Are there any echoes or exterior noises?

AV

- ☐ Are projectors and other AV equipment available and functional?
- ☐ Are there extra bulbs and other backups?
- ☐ Is there a light for the podium (if necessary)?

- ☐ Is the screen properly positioned?
- ☐ Are there electrical outlets for computer power?
- ☐ Is there an Internet connection or Wi-Fi available (if needed)?
- ☐ Are all cords and wires taped down?

ROOM SETUP

- ☐ Does the seating arrangement facilitate attention and interaction?
- ☐ Do you have the podiums, tables and easels you'll need?
- ☐ Can you and your team easily enter and exit room?

COMFORT LEVEL

- ☐ Spend time alone in the room.
- ☐ Visualize yourself making the presentation.
- ☐ Practice entering, standing, walking, sitting.
- ☐ Don't leave until you're comfortable with the space.

ALREADY
know the room?

Maybe the pitch is scheduled for your client's office or conference room. You've been there dozens of times. You know the room.

Get to know it better. Pay another visit or visualize the space.

- Where should you sit or stand?

- What's the best visual support to use, considering the room's lighting?

- What items in the room can you reference to build rapport or make points?

- Can you rearrange chairs and other furniture to better serve your presentation?

- Are there visual or sound distractions you must work around or try to eliminate?

DON'T JUST KNOW THE SPACE. OWN IT.

Laws _to keep in mind._

LAW OF LATENESS:
If you're presenting to a dozen people at 9 AM and one person is delayed, it will be the person who must make the final decision.

LAW OF CONNECTIONS:
The projector cable needed to connect with your computer is the only cable the venue doesn't have.

LAW OF LIQUIDS:
If coffee is spilled anywhere in the room, it will somehow wind up on your presentation materials.

LAW OF ACOUSTICS:
The probability of being heard is directly proportional to the stupidity of what you just said.

LAW OF PROJECTOR BULBS, SOUND SYSTEMS AND BINDER PAGES:
They will burn out, short out and fall out at the worst possible times.

LAW OF EXPOSURE:
If any zipper is down or buttonhole open, it will be yours.

LAW OF COMPARISONS:
When you try to prove to decision makers that the competitor's idea doesn't work, it will.

THREE *for the road.*

I'm on the road most weeks providing talks and seminars. These three items always travel with me. Consider packing them for your presentations.

DESK CLOCK: Few meeting rooms have wall clocks. And speakers glancing at their watches or cell phones look nervous. I pack a small clock with a large face and place it on the podium or table while I am presenting. It has kept me on time for years.

DUCT TAPE AND ARTIST'S TAPE: No matter how good the AV technicians are—even at large venues—there's always a cord to tape down or poster to tape up. Not to mention those emergency matters, like ripped bags, broken easels and wobbly projectors.

POST-IT NOTES: Minutes before a presentation, I'll often remember a point I've not rehearsed. Or a participant's question will spark another thought. In those cases, I stick Post-its on the table in front of me as reminders.

AN
actor's bag

Academy Award-winner Kate Winslet told *TIME* she prepares for every film by carrying a satchel containing a heavily annotated script, voice recorder, notebook, camera, pencil case, snapshots and other tools needed to master her role. When you're preparing pitches, what's in your bag?

PRESENTATION *checklist.*

☐ Pitch page (see page 123 for sample)

☐ Laptop computer

☐ Power cord

☐ Cables

☐ Slide advancer

☐ Visuals

☐ Printed summary

☐ Prototypes and samples

☐ Leave-behinds

☐ Notebook and pens

☐ Easel and whiteboard markers

☐ Business cards

☐ Post-its

☐ Tape

☐ Small desk clock

THEY CREATE,
but can they *sell*?

Managers sometimes assume team members will be fantastic presenters because they have fantastic ideas.

Not so fast.

The most creative person might be the least creative presenter. The person who flawlessly presents ideas in writing may struggle when presenting before a group. The smooth talker in the break room may be tongue-tied in the board room.

See your team members as audiences see them. Solicit outside opinions. Have dry runs. Assess strengths and weaknesses. Coach where you can. Get professional training when needed.

BENCH THOSE WHO SIMPLY CAN'T PITCH.

"We let the best presenters do the presenting," says Don McNeill of Digital Kitchen, "not necessarily the person who created the work. We don't bring anybody to client presentations who doesn't contribute or who doesn't know how to present."

READY *for the room.*

"We've all seen outstanding showmen present a mediocre idea that gets accepted over a remarkable idea simply because the presentation was better," says author and designer Stefan Mumaw.

How well we present the idea, Mumaw notes, is as important as the idea itself.

"One's ability to present is so important that it has attained its own term," he says. "We say creative people are 'great in the room' if they're strong presenters.

"We might describe a designer as having notable talent with good writing skills and an organic style, but then add he 'isn't that great in the room.' We're saying he develops and executes great ideas, but in meetings he can't convince clients the ideas are great."

Are you great in the room? Are you building skills to become great? What about other team members? Who's ready for the room?

Who's PITCHING TODAY?

When everybody works hard on an idea, everybody wants to join in on the pitch.

Sometimes you just have to say no. Find other ways to recognize those who don't make the cut. Hand out T-shirts. Throw a party.

But when you feel it's necessary for everybody to be there, here are three ways for less-capable presenters to get moments of glory:

1. GREETER. Pick the team member who connects one-on-one, but freezes in front of a group. Have her greet decision makers and make small talk before the pitch.

2. OPENER. Once decision makers are seated, the opener stands, introduces himself and says, "We're about ready to start. Is there anything we can get anyone before we do?" If someone has a request, perfect—the opener now has a task. If not, he says, "Wonderful, then Erin is ready to kick things off."

3. RESPONDERS. These team members answer one or more questions posed to them by your key presenter—and these questions have been carefully rehearsed. During his pitch, Thomas says, "Allie, I know you worked hard on this particular part of our idea. How do you see us rolling it out?" Allie's response is practiced to perfection—and if she's stage-shy, she gets to stay seated for her reply.

PITCH roster.

Taking your team to the presentation? Note who'll play each position.
(See the previous page for descriptions.)

KEY PRESENTER

SECONDARY PRESENTER(S)

GREETER(S)

OPENER

RESPONDER(S)

OTHER ROLES?

Test the Four Cs
ON YOUR PITCH.

After preparing your presentation, overlay the Four Cs to gauge its excellence.

CLARITY
Does the pitch clearly explain the idea? Will it connect with decision makers at their level?

CONTENT
Is it well researched? Does it address how the idea meets needs and objectives? Is it complete, yet concise?

CREATIVITY
Is the pitch interesting, compelling and informative? Does it contain showmanship and storytelling? Does it demonstrate the idea's originality and value?

CRAFT
Is the presentation well organized? Does it have a beginning, middle and end? Does it flow? Are visuals appropriate and meaningful? Have you practiced delivery?

WHAT'S
creative?
Before making your pitch, find out exactly what the client means by the word "creative," suggests ad man Paul Arden. It's probably different than your definition.

WHAT'S PLAYING
IN YOUR HEAD?

During talks and seminars, I often discuss what I call the Negative News Network, that insidious broadcast system playing inside our heads. Audience members always nod in unison, each person intimately familiar with the NNN's toxic signals.

The Negative News Network tells us we can't do things. That people will laugh. That we don't have what it takes to make winning presentations.

Dr. Daniel Amen, author of *Change Your Brain, Change Your Life*, labels these discouraging voices ANTs— Automatic Negative Thoughts.

If the Negative News Network plays in your mind during presentations, you'll exit the room with rejection. Pull the plug on NNN's oppressive programs when you're generating and selling ideas.

Unplug
THE NEGATIVE NEWS NETWORK.

If your internal broadcasting system is tuned in to negativity, switch it off before your presentation. Here's how:

1. WRITE IT ALL DOWN.
Write down exactly what the Negative News Network says to you. Study the words. See how unreasonable and unreliable they become when exposed to the light of day. Laugh at them. Burn the page.

2. TURN THE BEAT AROUND.
Talk to the Negative News Network rather than letting it talk to you. Call it stupid. Tell it to shut up. Shout at it. Give it hell.

3. EXERCISE.
The Negative News Network usually goes mute whenever physical activity shows up. Take a walk or go for a jog. Play a sport. Stroll through a park or mall. Get moving.

BEGGAR *or* BOOSTER?

Which one are you when heading into a pitch?

Boosters increase strength, value and reputation—for themselves and for decision makers. Boosters champion ideas. Add energy. Lift spirits.

Beggars, on the other hand, are impoverished. Deprived of strength. Takers rather than givers. They ask for sympathy. Plead for mercy.

Boosters have something to offer and know it. They're proud, confident, bold.

Beggars are victims and lack leverage.

When preparing to present, take an unbiased look at your idea. Does it allow you to enter the room as a booster? Or will you be forced to beg?

SOUNDS *of beggars.*

"This isn't exactly how I wanted the idea to turn out, but…"

"I THINK THIS IS A PRETTY GOOD IDEA, BUT…"

"This idea may not be what you're looking for, but…"

"I WANTED SOMETHING BETTER TO SHOW YOU, BUT…"

"I wish we had had more time, but…"

"I'll be happy to totally change this idea any way you like…"

And the ever popular:

"OH, PLEASE, PLEASE, PLEEEEASE…"

LACK CONFIDENCE?

FAKE IT.

Warming up for the 100-meter butterfly at the 2008 Olympics, Michael Phelps had low confidence. After winning six gold medals in earlier events, he felt exhausted.

"I've got nothing left," Phelps told his coach.

But Phelps didn't hang his head and slink away. He faked it. He walked confidently to the starting platform. Stood tall. Looked determined.

He hit the water and swam his heart out, staying neck and neck with rival Milorad Čavić. Approaching the finish line, Čavić tried gliding in, but Phelps took another half-stroke. The extra effort gave him the victory by one-hundredth of a second—the smallest possible margin.

Confidence restored, Phelps earned his record-breaking eighth gold medal the next day.

SOMETIMES THE BEST WAY TO FIND CONFIDENCE IS TO FAKE CONFIDENCE.

Sweep.

People love the idea of meeting Mr. or Ms. Right and being swept off their feet with inspiring conversation, entertaining stories and endearing emotion.

But if ten minutes into the first date they find themselves stuck with Mr. or Ms. Wrong, most people would just as soon call it a night and head home.

It's the same with decision makers. They want to be swept off their feet. Or sometimes they just want to sweep you out the door.

Here's the hard truth: Decision makers are often looking to say no. Saying no can be the easy way out. By saying no, they don't have to make hard choices. They don't have to spend money. They don't have to sell others on the idea.

That's why your presentation must be insightful, emotional and enjoyable. It's up to you to eliminate hard decisions. Show why their money's well spent. Explain how easily the idea can be sold to others.

DON'T LET THEM SWEEP YOU OUT THE DOOR. SWEEP THEM OFF THEIR FEET.

BODY WORK.

Feelings are communicated by body language more than by words. In fact, only seven percent of feelings are communicated with words, according to Jennifer Grau, an instructor at Cornell University's School of Industrial and Labor Relations.

Watch decision makers' body language for clues on how they feel about you and your ideas:

BORED: Drumming fingers. Swinging feet. Doodling. Looking around room or watching clock. Yawning, slouching or staring blankly.

INTERESTED: Stillness. Ignoring distractions. Leaning forward. Returning eye contact. Arms or hands open. Slow nodding. Responsive words.

CLOSE-MINDED: Crossed arms or legs. Looking downward or away from you.

CONSIDERING: Steepled hands, usually touching chin or lips. Stroking of chin, cheek or other parts of face. Intense gaze. Pursed lips.

INSECURE: Biting nails. Fondling hair. Lack of eye contact. Clutching objects (notebooks, folders, etc.) to front of body.

Watch YOUR BODY.

Decision makers pick up signals from your body language. So pay close attention to your visual expressions:

1. RELAX SHOULDERS. Otherwise, you'll look tense or nervous.

2. SIT OR STAND STRAIGHT. But stay relaxed, not stiff.

3. SIT BACK IN YOUR CHAIR. Perching on the edge of your seat makes you look nervous—and makes decision makers uneasy.

4. LEAN IN. But not so far that you appear off balance or seem needy.

5. DON'T CROSS ARMS OR LEGS. This makes you look guarded or defensive.

6. DON'T CLUTCH PAPERS OR OBJECTS IN FRONT OF CHEST. This also makes you look defensive.

7. HAVE EYE CONTACT. But don't stare.

8. SMILE AND LAUGH OFTEN. But don't lock a smile on your face or laugh too quickly and loudly.

9. NOD. But not so frequently that you look like a bobblehead doll.

10. WATCH YOUR HANDS. Gesture, but otherwise keep hands calm. Don't fidget with clothing, hair, pens, paper clips and other objects. And don't mindlessly scratch face, neck or arm.

11. RESPECT PERSONAL SPACE. Don't stand too close.

12. STAY AWARE OF YOUR FACE. Avoid grimaces, frowns and frozen expressions.

TURN HEADS
THE RIGHT WAY.

Where you stand or sit during a pitch could affect how you're perceived by decision makers.

When right-handed people look to their right, they experience feelings of comfort and calm. Looking to the left, these people often feel fear and anxiety.

"Ultimately, those feelings, both good and bad, become connected with the speaker," says Dr. Kevin Hogan, a body language expert.

If you stand or sit to the right of a right-handed person, he will tend to like you significantly more than if you were on his left, according to Dr. Hogan's research, which is supported by similar studies conducted by Dr. Fredric Schiffer.

If your decision maker is right-handed, try sitting or standing to her right when talking or making pitches. Stand to the left when presenting to a left-handed person.

STAY *in the now.*

> "*Walking into a presenta-
> tion room, I'm thinking
> about getting out of
> that room.*"

After a participant in my seminar made
this confession, others made similar
admissions. It's a common feeling.

We're often hungry to hurry out because
we're nervous going in. But even when
confident, we'll sometimes burn up the
road, eager to get the OK and exit. This
haste handicaps us, because we miss
relationship-building opportunities and
cues about the decision maker's needs.

People pick up on this hurriedness.
They sense it's more about us than
them. About taking rather than giving.

"Early in my career, I had more of an
agenda," says writer Sally Hogshead.
"Now I focus more on the conversation.
I ask more questions and spend more
time listening."

Pitch page.

Complete this page and then review it just before entering the meeting room.
Keep it in front of you for opening conversations and during your presentation.

IDEA

DECISION MAKER

Decision maker profile (quick facts about the decision maker—responsibilities, interests, hobbies, college, heroes, names of spouse/partner, kids, pets, etc.)

Opening questions (icebreakers and conversation starters)

Probing questions (to gain insights)

Key points (points you absolutely must make before leaving room)

Outline (intended flow for the presentation)

6

How to present
A POWERFUL PITCH.

"The audience only pays attention as long
as you know where you are going."

—Philip Crosby, ACTOR

LET A WORLD LEADER PITCH
your *next* idea.

Sir Winston Churchill was a world-class speaker and salesman for ideas.

Here are his five guidelines for successful presentations:

1. HAVE ONE THEME.
Develop a concise, focused, overarching theme.

2. MAKE A STRONG START.
Grab the decision maker's attention right from the beginning.

3. USE SIMPLE LANGUAGE.
Your words should not be simplistic, but they must be clear and conversational.

4. PAINT PICTURES.
Plant images in the minds of decision makers so they visualize your solutions.

5. ADD DRAMA.
Build anticipation and excitement that fit your ideas and audiences.

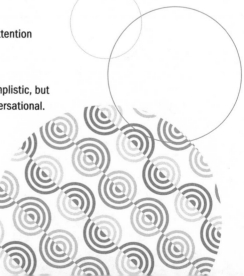

1. HAVE ONE THEME.

I sat down for a financial planner's presentation. After fifteen minutes, I yearned for an ejection seat.

This guy was all over the place. He started by talking about stocks and bonds. Then he jumped to life insurance. A quick hop to disability coverage. Back to stocks and bonds. And, wait, let's not forget estate planning...

There was no central thread. Just aim a fire hose in my direction and hope something hits. Instead, he drowned my interest with disconnected data.

Needless to say, I didn't sign up. He knew his stuff, no doubt about it. But without a central theme linked to my needs, he sounded like Charlie Brown's teacher: "Waa waa waa... waa waa..."

Study the decision maker's needs. Connect with a solid theme.

Know what you want
TO HAVE HAPPEN.

When preparing to pitch, we usually start by asking ourselves: "What am I going to say?"

A better first question would be: "What do I want to have happen?"

Sure, you want to sell the idea. But how do you see that happening? What reactions do you want? What questions would you like answered? What interactions? Action steps? Timelines? Approvals?

When people presented to Walt Disney, he would ask, "What's the end frame?" He viewed life through a cartoonist's eyes, with the end frame as the payoff.

What's the end frame of your presentation? What do you want to have happen?

KNOW THE ANSWER, AND YOU'LL KNOW YOUR THEME.

KNOW WHAT YOU WANT
TO SAY.

After Harold Macmillan made his first address to Britain's House of Commons, Winston Churchill had this to say:

"Harold, when you rose you didn't know what you were going to say, when you were speaking you didn't know what you were saying, and when you finished you didn't know what you had said."

Know what you want to say, and say it. DON'T RAMBLE.

HELP CLIENTS
visualize your ideas.

"When presenting, we strive to create an experience and help clients visualize ideas as reality," says DJ Stout, a partner at Pentagram.

When Lexington, Kentucky, asked Pentagram to develop an identity reflecting the Bluegrass Region's personality, Stout and Michael Bierut conjured up a mythical mascot, Big Lex. To create Big Lex, they took the majestic horse in Edward Troye's 1868 portrait of the great racehorse Lexington and switched its color to blue.

"When we showed city leaders Troye's horse colored bright blue, their initial resistance was evident," says Stout. "But then we displayed examples of ads and billboards—and a prototype of Big Lex as a small model that could be sold in gift shops.

"We also showed how Big Lex could be a mascot, with a person wearing a blue horse suit and educating school kids about the racehorse Lexington. The decision makers began to visually experience where we were going with the idea. Before long, everybody in the room was suggesting ways Big Lex could promote the city."

Helping clients visualize success is customary at Pentagram, says Stout. "I remember Paula Scher presenting packaging ideas for a technology product. In the conference room, she had shelves stacked with product boxes of competitors. Paula opened her presentation by placing an unadorned orange box on the shelves.

"'Look how your box would attract attention,' she said. Then she slowly applied graceful graphics to the box, helping clients visualize how refinement and simplicity would pull in buyers and easily explain the box's contents."

FOCUS = SACRIFICE

"Too many presentations look like they have been put together by lawyers," says Al Ries, branding expert and co-author of *War in the Boardroom*. "The presenter takes all the reasons why a client should buy and lists them one by one, hoping one will hit a home run. It seldom works."

Ries notes that even some lawyers have learned the lesson of focus. "Take Johnnie Cochran in the O.J. Simpson case," he says. "'If the glove doesn't fit, you must acquit.'"

Powerful brands are built by focusing, Ries points out. "Federal Express became the largest U.S. air cargo carrier by focusing on overnight delivery," he says. "BMW became the world's largest-selling luxury car brand by focusing on driving. Target became a worthy competitor to Walmart by focusing on well-designed merchandise.

"The secret of a good presentation is sacrifice. In other words, focus."

Fast pitch.

"If I can't pitch a book to my wife in about three sentences, I'm in trouble," author John Grisham told interviewer Charlie Rose. "I spend a lot of time with the story to make sure I'm focused on a theme.

"Take my book *The Firm*. One day in the kitchen, I said to my wife, 'I've got an idea for a book. This young lawyer joins a law firm, and once you join that law firm, you can never leave it because it's secretly owned by the Mafia.'

"My wife stopped what she was doing and said, 'Say that again.' I repeated the sentence. And she said, 'That's a good book.'"

BREATH TEST.

IF YOU CAN'T DESCRIBE YOUR CONCEPT WITHOUT HAVING TO TAKE A BREATH, YOU PROBABLY HAVEN'T NAILED YOUR THEME.

Yes, it's possible—filmmakers do it all the time with their thirty-second "high concept" pitches for two-hour movies. See if you can identify the following films from their one-sentence themes:

1. Scientists clone dinosaurs to populate a theme park, which suffers a security breakdown and releases the dinosaurs.

2. An unemployed actor disguises himself as a woman to get a soap-opera role.

3. A police chief, a scientist and a grizzled sailor set out to kill a shark that is menacing a seaside community.

4. A woman and daughter open a chocolate shop in a French village and shake the town's rigid morality.

5. An insurance salesman discovers his entire life is actually a TV show.

6. An eight-year-old is accidentally left behind when his family goes on vacation, and he has to defend his home against idiotic burglars.

1. *Jurassic Park* 2. *Tootsie* 3. *Jaws* 4. *Chocolat* 5. *The Truman Show* 6. *Home Alone*

Focus.

IF I HAD TO PITCH THIS IDEA IN ONE OR TWO SENTENCES, I WOULD SAY:

HERE ARE THE THREE MAIN POINTS I WANT TO MAKE DURING MY PRESENTATION:

1.

2.

3.

HERE'S THE THEME I'LL USE TO UNITE AND FOCUS MY PRESENTATION:

LEAVE CHAOS
at the door.

We often have problems presenting creative ideas because of a chumminess with chaos. After all, creativity can be a wild and crazy affair.

We sometimes try pitching ideas the same way we created them. And in our ramblings, we lose credibility and clarity.

The way we create may look like this:

But the way we present should look like this:

I'm not saying idea pitches should be dull and didactic. God forbid. Pull out the fireworks and crank up the Ferris wheel if they'll rouse the room and illuminate ideas. Dare to show bold creations. Playing it safe is for wimps.

But organize your thoughts before making pitches. Present your idea in a logical flow so you can be easily understood.

MEET DECISION MAKERS ON THEIR MENTAL TURF. GENTLY GUIDE THEM TO YOUR WORLD.

"Be regular and orderly in your life, so that you may be violent and original in your work."

—Gustave Flaubert, WRITER

Fill in the blanks.

When meeting one-on-one with a decision maker, try a fill-in-the-blanks pitch. I used this technique out of necessity years ago when a printing error left several pages of my presentation partially or completely blank.

I've turned to it several times since, always with good results. And Seth Godin has blogged about a similar process.

How the fill-in-the-blanks pitch works:

1. PREPARE A HANDHELD, FLIP-CHART-STYLE PRESENTATION. USE SIMPLE VISUALS AND WORDS TO GUIDE AND EMPHASIZE KEY POINTS.

2. DELETE BITS OF IMPORTANT INFORMATION ON EACH PAGE—YOU MAY EVEN DECIDE TO HAVE A FEW SHEETS WITH ONLY EMPTY BOXES OR LINES.

3. PRINT ON QUALITY PAPER AND BIND IN A WAY THAT PAGES EASILY TURN.

4. AT THE IDEA PITCH, SIT BESIDE THE DECISION MAKER WITH THE PRINTED PIECE AS YOUR SUPPORT CENTER. GO THROUGH PAGE BY PAGE, WRITING IN MISSING INFORMATION WHILE DISCUSSING YOUR IDEA.

This interactive process adds spontaneity—and glues the decision maker's attention to your main messages.

PAUSE
before you start.

A few years ago, I saw Edward Norton and four other actors participate in a panel discussion at the Directors Guild in Manhattan.

The panel quickly adopted a rotation, with each actor briefly commenting on film-related topics. But whenever it was Norton's turn to speak, he would pause and study the audience. We waited on his words.

Norton's comments were no more profound than those of other panelists. But his pauses caused him to come across as the group's sage.

For your next pitch, pause a few seconds before actually starting your presentation. Lock eyes on audience members. Mentally rehearse your first sentence. Build anticipation.

ONCE YOU HAVE THEIR FULL ATTENTION, BEGIN.

2. Make a
STRONG START.

Tom Duncan entered a presentation room with a power drill in each hand. One was made by his company, Positec Power Tool Group, the other by a competitor. He placed the drills on a table and used a screwdriver to began taking them apart.

He instantly grabbed the attention of decision makers. And they followed him as he pointed out differences in construction and design.

Showmanship helps provide strong starts. Sometimes this may simply be a remarkable sentence. Soliciting for a contribution, a nonprofit executive nabbed my attention by opening with a favorite Gandhi quote: "Anything you do will seem insignificant, but it's important that you do it."

When you begin a presentation, your decision maker's mind is probably elsewhere—worrying about bills, remembering last night's game, pondering tonight's dinner.

START STRONGLY. CAPTURE ATTENTION.

Opening lines.

Novelists recognize the value of strong starts. If readers aren't intrigued by the first sentence, they'll likely forego subsequent sentences.

Here are a few classic, irresistible first lines from literature. Each one entices the reader to keep going. Let these inspire you to make strong starts.

"All children, except one, grow up."

—J.M. Barrie, *PETER PAN*

"He was an old man who fished alone in a skiff in the Gulf Stream and he had gone eighty-four days now without taking a fish."

—Ernest Hemingway,
THE OLD MAN AND THE SEA

"There were 117 psychoanalysts on the Pan Am flight to Vienna and I'd been treated by at least six of them."

—Erica Jong, *FEAR OF FLYING*

"On a cold blowy February day a woman is boarding the ten a.m. flight to London, followed by an invisible dog."

—Alison Lurie, *FOREIGN AFFAIRS*

"If you really want to hear about it, the first thing you'll probably want to know is where I was born, and what my lousy childhood was like, and how my parents were occupied and all before they had me, and all that David Copperfield kind of crap, but I don't feel like going into it, if you want to know the truth."

—J.D. Salinger, *THE CATCHER IN THE RYE*

SIX WAYS
TO START A PITCH.

After chitchat and rapport-building, you're ready to begin your presentation. Here are six options for kicking it off:

1. TELL A STORY. Fill it with human interest and relate it to your idea.

"Let me begin by telling you about the time my husband thought he would save money by changing the oil in our cars..."

2. ASK A QUESTION. Elicit an answer that leads in to your idea.

"I've been noticing the needs our new customers have for related services in the first year. What are your thoughts about those opportunities?"

3. STATE A FACT. Again, tie it in to your idea—and ideally spotlight your research.

"I was astonished to discover in our research that half of all dog owners are slowly killing their pets through unintentional malnutrition..."

4. USE A PROVOCATIVE QUOTE. Possibly even play back one of the decision maker's comments or favorite sayings.

"You made a statement at last fall's retreat that really stuck with me. You said, 'If we don't make our customers happy, somebody else will'..."

5. CONNECT WITH OBJECTIVES. Acknowledge goals and objectives.

"When we first talked about this challenge, you said the number one objective of any solution had to be retaining existing employees..."

6. TALK PEER-TO-PEER. This could be a sensitive tactic, so save it for the perfect moment and the right idea.

"You and I have sat down and looked at lots of ideas together, John. But I have to say, I'm drawn more to this idea than any we've ever discussed..."

ONE OPENING LINE
not to use.

Never start your presentation by saying, "You're going to love this idea."

Kick off with that line and you'll kick-start skepticism. The decision maker will think, *"Oh, yeah?"* or *"Wanna bet?"* You'll be an easy target, a clown perched over a dunking tank.

I learned my lesson with this one on my first job out of college. We had developed a new corporate identity program, and I was dispatched to tell a plant manager he would need to replace all of his facility's signage.

In my youthful exuberance, it didn't occur that the gruff, overworked manager might have a few other things on his mind, such as production quotas, union battles and on-the-job injuries. Switching out signs likely ranked dead last on his priority list.

"You're going to love these signs we've created for you," I said.

Looking up from a mess of thick reports on his desk, he stared at me for a long time. "No, what I would love," he said, "is to send you back to headquarters with those fancy signs stuck up your tail."

That's the last time I tried that line.

IF YOUR STORY IS ABOUT A BEAR,
START TALKING *about the bear.*

At some point, all journalists receive advice like this from professors and editors:

"If you're writing about seeing a bear while walking in the woods, get to the bear. Don't start with shopping for a pair of hiking boots."

They're telling verbose writers not to begin at the beginning of the story, but in the middle—where there's action and drama.

That's also good advice for idea pitches. Don't put decision makers to sleep with long-winded details about how you developed your idea.

START WITH CONTENT THAT CAPTURES ATTENTION.

"When you advertise fire extinguishers, open with the fire."

—David Ogilvy

Show problem,
THEN SHOW SOLUTION.

Working to boost a client's impact at trade shows, we called in an exhibits designer to show his ideas.

He flipped on the projector. But instead of parading his work, he flashed images of an exhibitor's nightmare. Overcrowded space. Ineffective signage. Dim lighting. Ratty carpets. Messy displays. Inadequate storage. Exposed cables.

He had done his homework. To varying degrees, these were problems with the client's current exhibits. The images made us feel those problems.

With strategically arranged vignettes, he next showed how his ideas solved those problems. An open floor plan. Prominent signage. Warm lighting. Cushioned flooring. Organized displays. Efficient storage. Concealed cables.

By the time he revealed his total design, we were already sold. He knew the problems. He created solutions. And his pitch helped us understand both.

"Ask yourself what makes your idea the perfect solution for your client," says author Sally Hogshead.

"Demonstrate why your solution is the best one for their most pressing needs. That way, you're not presenting a vague idea—you're sharing a powerful tool."

WHAT'S THE problem?

DATE:

IDEA:

Here's the problem:

How I'll show the problem in my presentation:

THE POWER
of because.

Leverage your pitch statements with logical justifications.

For example, say:

"I'm proposing this idea because..."

"We did research on this because..."

"We selected this color because..."

*"We feel this language is right for your
customers because..."*

*"This idea is worth a large portion of the
budget because..."*

*"We need to implement this idea as quickly
as possible because..."*

Don't do DULL.

Tempting decision makers is easy when ideas are sexy and exotic. But what about pitching a concept that's valuable but less glamorous?

One story that inspires me is Publix Super Markets and their store brand of aluminum foil. That's right—boring aluminum foil.

Publix designers turned packaging of everyday aluminum foil into something inventive, inviting and fun. They created a clean, crisp box featuring small foil sculptures—turtles, deer and other animals.

Shoppers couldn't resist reaching for the clever package. Some even asked store managers for instructions on how to create the sculptures.

If Publix can make aluminum foil enticing, you can make your concept alluring for a presentation—perhaps by placing it in an inventive container or concealing it in an interesting way until the big reveal.

I've seen printed documents nestled in bird cages and tucked in empty soup cans. Prototypes pulled from mailboxes and baked inside bread. Renderings hidden behind velvet curtains and hanging from strings of white lights.

HOW CAN YOU PACKAGE YOUR CONCEPT TO MAKE IT MORE SEDUCTIVE?

On the line.

Orbiting the Giant Hairball is one of my favorite creativity books. The author, Gordon MacKenzie, was Hallmark's in-resident creative guru for many years, and I've often heard about his "clothesline" presentation technique.

"On the stage behind Gordon were giant index cards on a clothesline," says Alan Black, author of *Broken Crayons*, who told me of being in the audience at a MacKenzie presentation. "On the cards were sketches representing stories he was ready to tell to make various points.

"The cards were numbered, and MacKenzie asked that we shout a number, and he would tell the story related to the card. He also said if anyone was ready for him to wrap up, that person merely had to shout the number thirteen. MacKenzie

would immediately end his presentation with a final story.

"Only one stipulation—the person who yelled 'thirteen' would be required to stand up, say his or her name and tell everybody how to reach him or her—in case other audience members wanted to complain about not getting to hear the entire presentation."

SHOWMANSHIP DOESN'T REQUIRE BIG BUCKS. JUST BIG IMAGINATION.

PITCH TIPS
FROM A MUSIC HALL.

If you find yourself captivated by a comedian, singer or other entertainer, study his or her methods. That's what Jim Bolshevik, DDB West creative director, did one night at an East Village music hall.

"This musician, Jason Anderson, didn't go near the stage," says Bolshevik. "He just stood in the middle of the room, playing his acoustic guitar and singing. He made eye contact with everyone, one by one.

"He asked us to stand. He asked us to sing along. We all gathered in a circle around him, and he said some pretty hippy-dippy stuff about being there in the moment. But we were. It was fantastic.

"Jason made an impact because he immediately killed our expectations. We were thinking, 'OK, what the heck is this guy going to do?'

"He engaged us. And it wasn't just the normal chatter from the stage. He was down with us. He connected with us—not as a crowd, but as individuals.

"And, he got us to participate.

"Leaving the club, my buddy and I had the same thought: We should get this guy to come play at the agency. Watching him beats any class you could ever have on presentation skills."

Nodders
AND NAPPERS.

I speak to audiences large and small. In any size audience, I'll always spot at least one Nodder and one Napper.

Nodder nods in agreement throughout the talk. And Napper? Well, he (sorry, guys, it's almost always a he) can be counted on to nap—or appear as if his mind has left for the golf course, beach or bar.

Long live both Nodder and Napper, because I need them.

To the Nodder I look when wanting reassurance. "Yes, I'm still with you," Nodder seems to say. "Keep going."

Nodder also serves as my canary in the coal mine. If she quits nodding, there's trouble in paradise. Maybe I've let myself get caught up in some lengthy example or unrelated tangent. Time to correct course.

She's nodding again? Wonderful—back in business.

I also closely watch Napper. If I capture his interest, I'm assured of having the rest of the audience.

Make eye contact with everybody in your presentation. But pick out the Nodder and the Napper— and let them help you make a stronger pitch.

3. USE SIMPLE
language.

Read this sentence from a product brochure:

"We offer a financially-reasonable, high-performance USB high speed-based pod with functionality as a deep sample buffer logic analyzer and signal."

Translation?

Decipher this sentence from an academic journal:

"If, for a while, the ruse of desire is calculable for the uses of discipline, soon the repetition of guilt, justification, pseudo-scientific theories, superstition, spurious authorities, and classifications can be seen as the desperate effort to 'normalize' formally the disturbance of a discourse of splitting that violates the rational, enlightened claims of its enunciatory modality."

Huh?

Extremes, to be sure. But we've all struggled through copy and endured presentations filled with fifty-dollar words and obscure technical terms.

Those messengers strive to impress, but instead audiences react with confusion, frustration or indifference.

Keep your presentations clear and conversational, free of technical lingo, insider language and lofty words.

WITHOUT BEING SIMPLE-MINDED, BE SIMPLE.

"Everything should be made as simple as possible, but no simpler."
—Albert Einstein

"Perfection is reached not when there's nothing left to add, but when there's nothing left to take away."

—Antoine de Saint-Exupéry,
AUTHOR AND POET

"WHEN IN DOUBT,

reduce."

That's a popular chef's axiom on the heat reduction of broth, wine and other liquids to prepare sauces.

It's also good advice for preparing presentations.

If you're wondering whether your presentation is overly wordy, it probably is. If you're worried you might have too many visuals, you probably do. If you're concerned you won't be able to hold your client's attention for the length of the pitch you've prepared, you probably can't.

IN SHORT, IF YOU'RE IN DOUBT ABOUT YOUR PRESENTATION'S BULK, REDUCE.

"I wish you had talked longer" are words you'll never hear from clients.

153

STAND TALL,
talk short.

In 1863, Pennsylvania prepared to dedicate a cemetery for soldiers killed in the Battle of Gettysburg.

Famed orator Edward Everett was asked to be the main speaker. He immediately requested the ceremony be postponed three weeks to give him more time to write his speech.

President Abraham Lincoln was also invited, almost as an afterthought.

Everett spoke for two hours, delivering more than 13,500 words.

Lincoln spoke for two minutes and delivered 272 words.

Nobody remembers Everett's talk. But Lincoln's Gettysburg Address is celebrated as one of America's finest speeches.

WHEN CHOOSING BETWEEN LONGER OR SHORTER, CHOOSE SHORTER.

KNOW THREE Ps.

For winning pitches, know these three Ps:

PEOPLE: Know as much as possible about stakeholders who would be touched by your idea. Decision makers. Customers. Employees. And know yourself—your best presentation style, your strengths and your areas to improve.

PRODUCT: The idea you're about to pitch is your product, your baby. Know every detail. Be passionate about it. And be ready to respond to objections.

PRESENTATION: Know your pitch as well as your favorite song. Refine it. Focus it. Enrich it. Rehearse it.

What you like best
MAY NOT BE *what works best.*

My wife and I decided to redecorate a room and hired an interior designer.

She looked at the existing room and began offering ideas. But with each suggestion, we countered with our fondness for the furniture or art she wanted to move out.

"Look, just because you like something doesn't mean it belongs in this room," she said. "If you want to fill the room with stuff just because you like it, no problem. But don't expect to have a well-designed room."

Well, we listened and ended up with a room we love. And I gained another excellent piece of advice: Just because you like something doesn't automatically mean it belongs—if you're seeking the best.

Just because you like a type font doesn't automatically mean it belongs in the brochure you're designing.

Just because you like a sentence doesn't automatically mean it belongs in the article you're writing.

And just because you like a story or visual doesn't automatically mean it belongs in the pitch you're preparing.

What we like best isn't always what works best if we're seeking the best.

DON'T NUMB
WITH NUMBERS.

Statistics can build credibility. But not if you bombard decision makers with truckloads of facts and figures.

Speechwriter James Humes recommends three Rs—reduce, round and relate—when dealing with statistics.

REDUCE
Less is more when it comes to numbers—pick one or two statistics that hammer home why decision makers should approve your idea.

ROUND
Round off statistics. Rather than saying "Seventy-four percent of end users prefer this type of packaging," say "Three out of four customers prefer this type of packaging." Symbolic photos and drawings also add clarity.

RELATE
Relate the statistic to a story or illustration: "My idea for this promotion costs one-third of what it would cost to buy a single thirty-second commercial on a local TV station..." or "If only one customer out of a hundred acts on this solicitation, we'll realize a return of investment of more than 20 percent..."

CREATE
memorable lines.

> "May the Force be with you."
>
> "Go ahead, make my day."
>
> "Frankly, my dear, I don't give a damn."

These movie lines are dozens of years old. But, like "E.T. phone home" and "Show me the money," they're part of our mental furniture.

Can you create memorable lines for your pitches—something decision makers can't forget and want to remember?

A writing-instrument salesman showed my catalog buyer a pen with a light in its barrel and said, "This pen captures those two-in-the-morning ideas."

He captured her imagination, so she included the pen—and we, of course, captured his line for our marketing copy.

Similes and metaphors also help nail memorable lines. In explaining how Virgin America airline is more than just a way to get from one place to another, Porter Gale, Virgin's marketing vice president, said the experience is "like flying in an iPod."

Like flying in an iPod. Can you invent an equally graphic line to sell your idea?

RECOGNIZE these lines?

Take a break and match these lines with their films.
Appreciate the power and endurance of memorable lines.

1. "I'LL HAVE WHAT SHE'S HAVING."

2. *"You had me at hello."*

3. "I'M WALKING HERE!"

4. *"Nobody puts Baby in a corner."*

5. "IS IT SAFE?"

6. "TOGA! TOGA!"

7. *"You can't handle the truth!"*

8. "I'M GOING TO MAKE HIM AN OFFER HE CAN'T REFUSE."

9. *"Stella! Hey, Stella!"*

10. *"We'll always have Paris."*

a. *Midnight Cowboy*

b. *A Streetcar Named Desire*

c. *Casablanca*

d. *Jerry Maguire*

e. *When Harry Met Sally*

f. *Dirty Dancing*

g. *Animal House*

h. *Marathon Man*

i. *A Few Good Men*

j. *The Godfather*

1e, 2d, 3a, 4f, 5h, 6g, 7i, 8j, 9b, 10c

Voice

OF CONFIDENCE.

It's not just what you say. It's also how you deliver the words. Pay attention to volume, pitch and speaking speed.

VOLUME: How loudly do you speak? A presenter with a weak, low-volume voice is perceived as lacking confidence. Conversely, a strong, vibrant voice oozes confidence. But resist cranking the volume too high—save shouting for ball games and rock concerts.

PITCH: Are you holding one note or varying your voice? People who change pitch to match what they're saying are perceived as energetic, expressive and confident. People maintaining the same pitch appear monotonous, tired and dull.

SPEAKING SPEED: Are your words flying down the highway or chugging in the slow lane? Or are you cruising along at a comfortable pace? People who speak too slowly or hesitate too often lose their audiences. And the same for people who speak so fast they sound like cattle auctioneers. Speak fast enough to maintain interest, but slow enough for clarity.

watch how
YOU PHRASE THINGS.

Look at these statements:

"This photo is eerie, but it works for our idea."

"This photo works for our idea, but it is eerie."

The same words in different arrangements result in different connotations. Be sure your phrasing doesn't convey unintended doubt and open doors for second-guessing.

"*Hopefully maybe*
THIS IS SORT OF A PRETTY GOOD IDEA."

You ask the waiter for his opinion of the risotto al funghi:

"I kind of think it's a pretty good dish and you might possibly like it."

Ready to order?

Or ask the ophthalmologist if you're a good candidate for Lasik eye surgery:

"I sort of believe it might help and hopefully you would see better."

Eager for the procedure?

In daily conversations, we all use qualifiers and disclaimers like "sort of," "I think," "I hope," and "pretty good." But pluck these from presentations. Such words make you appear noncommittal and insecure.

DISCLAIMERS
AND QUALIFIERS.

1. Using an audio or video recorder, capture yourself presenting an idea. If you can record an actual presentation, go for it. Otherwise, do a dress rehearsal—just as if you were presenting to the client—with visual aids and, if possible, an audience (spouse, co-worker, the family dog).

2. Carefully listen to yourself.

3. List your pet qualifiers and disclaimers (such as "maybe," pretty good," "probably," "sort of," "I hope" and "I think"):

4. Now that you are aware of them, work on eliminating them.

4. PAINT *pictures.*

Few of us have the oratory skills of Martin Luther King. And even if we were in Dr. King's league, his grand style would rarely be right for our pitches.

But by studying Dr. King's words, we can appreciate the value of speaking in pictures. Consider these lines from his "I Have a Dream" speech:

> "...every hill and mountain shall be made low, the rough places will be made plain and the crooked places will be made straight..."

> "...little black boys and black girls will be able to join hands with little white boys and white girls as sisters and brothers..."

> "...lift our nation from the quicksands of racial injustice to the solid rock of brotherhood..."

> "...justice rolls down like waters, and righteousness like a mighty stream..."

WITH DR. KING'S WORDS, WE DON'T JUST HEAR, WE SEE.

Show, DON'T TELL.

*Convert the following "tell" sentences to "show" sentences
(as demonstrated in the example):*

TELL: "This toothbrush's design will appeal to small kids."

SHOW: "My niece Megan giggled and grabbed this toothbrush the second she saw it."

TELL: "This communications plan will help educate company employees."

SHOW:

TELL: "Our media efforts will convey the scope of the mission to target markets."

SHOW:

TELL: "The networking event provides corporate outreach to high-end audiences."

SHOW:

PROTOTYPE.

Bring ideas to life. Show pitch books, prototypes, drafts, models, sketches and samples. Use examples from other firms if they have a desired look or voice.

And don't hold everything back for a final presentation. Early prototyping helps determine if you're on track with decision makers.

"These days we tend to share ideas in a more raw state," says Hallmark's Trish Berrong. "Our clients then feel no pressure to be super articulate in describing what they like and don't like. Hierarchy goes away, and we're just people working together toward a solution."

IDEO, a widely acclaimed product-development firm, calls prototyping "the shorthand of innovation."

PROBLEMS GET FIXED BEFORE
THEY BECOME DEAL BREAKERS.

BRING SEEDS
to life.

"We bring idea seeds to life so people can respond to them more viscerally," says Lisa Maulhardt, head writer and partner at Stone Yamashita Partners. "Whether it's a strategy, vision or creative idea, we strongly believe in the necessity of seeing before teams can believe, think and act differently."

"We help them see a new reality so they can figure out what to do next."

Stone Yamashita Partners uses creative techniques to sprout idea seeds in client presentations.

"Sometimes it's building out a prototype of a retail environment," Maulhardt says. "Other times it's mocking up web interfaces for consumer services, or writing future newspaper articles reflecting the change a client is considering.

Tell a story.

"Tell me a story" are four of the most important words in our language, says novelist Pat Conroy. Storytelling connects us as humans, reminding us of our common bonds.

That's why storytelling is jet fuel for presentations.

"There's something primal about stories," says Lisa Maulhardt of Stone Yamashita Partners. "Aural, verbal, written and visual stories help us make sense of our world. I've heard that selling is the same as leading. Since telling a story is a form of leading, presentations benefit from storytelling.

By using stories in presentations, we're enticing people to follow along. Stories say, 'Come this way, take that hill, believe in something better.'"

The story's HERO.

"I once heard Nelson Mandela talk to a group of very influential folks about investing in South Africa," film producer Peter Guber told *Best Life*. "Not once did he mention rates of return, gross profits or tax benefits."

Mandela simply told the story of his country. "Sure, the investors would pat their pockets," said Guber, "but that's not what they were talking about when they left the room. They were abuzz with the impact their investment would have on future generations.

"THAT'S THE KEY TO EFFECTIVE STORYTELLING. MAKE YOUR LISTENERS FEEL NOT ONLY GENEROUS, BUT ALSO LIKE THE HEROES OF A GREAT STORY."

PITCH = STORY

"A pitch is a story," says Stefan Mumaw, designer and author. "When we pitch a client, we are telling the story of the idea—but, more importantly, we are telling the story of what the idea means to their customers."

The deeper the story, explains Mumaw, the deeper the connection to the idea.

"Our agency pitched a sporting-goods retailer on an ad campaign about the passion tennis players have for the game," he says. "But we wanted to notch up the passion to an addiction."

Mumaw's team pitched the idea by telling a story about an addicted tennis player. "We told what he does, how he thinks," he says. "At the end of our story, we attached the client's product to the same principle.

"Without the story, our campaign idea lacked depth or life. The campaign tells a story to the consumer, of course. But without us telling that story to the client in the pitch, the idea would have never reached the consumer."

RIDE *the carousel.*

There's a scene in the TV show *Mad Men* where Don Draper pitches Kodak executives about the company's revolutionary new slide projector.

Kodak called the projector's slide holder a "wheel." Draper changes the name to a "carousel," describing it as a childlike time machine.

With tender words and family snapshots, Draper uses the carousel to tell a personal, visual story that renders everyone speechless, a story that passionately conveys the spirit of his idea:

"This device... isn't a spaceship, it's a time machine. It goes backwards, forwards. It takes us to a place where we ache to go again. It's not called the Wheel. It's called the Carousel. It lets us travel the way a child travels. Around and around and back home again, to a place where we know we are loved."

"Draper communicates the very essence of the idea in his own life," says designer Stefan Mumaw. "He tells a personal story. If we want our clients to be passionate about our idea, we have to first own that passion."

WHAT'S YOUR *story?*

YOUR IDEA:

PROBLEM IT SOLVES:

STORIES TO BRING ISSUES AND IDEAS TO LIFE:

1.

2.

3.

Share *yourself.*

In one of my workshops, a creative director told how she punches up pitches with stories about her experiences in community theater.

"I talk about when I forgot my lines in *The Glass Menagerie* to underscore the importance of remembering customer service," she said. "I describe being in a scene with rambling dialogue to punctuate the need for focused copy."

Sharing personal episodes helps illustrate your points—and adds a human touch. Not self-serving monologues, of course. Just a couple of short stories from sports, hobbies, everyday life.

The creative director's examples worked especially well because they were also self-deprecating. Some of the best lines in my talks—ones I use over and again—are small stories where I poke fun at myself.

"I always laugh the hardest at the stuff you see in day-to-day life," says actor Luke Wilson. "It's great when somebody can tell a joke that really makes you laugh hard, but to see some kind of personal interaction that no one could write is so good."

PEOPLE LIKE PEOPLE WHO APPEAR HUMAN. AND WHO DON'T TAKE THEMSELVES SO SERIOUSLY.

KEEP THEIR ATTENTION
focused on you.

Yes, presentations are about how the idea helps solve decision makers' problems. And by all means, involve your audience, have conversations, encourage interaction.

But at the end of the day, it's your job to explain the idea's value.

So stay front and center. Don't let your own support tools pull attention away from you.

Beware of:

- cluttered slides.

- long copy you read—or that you ask decision makers to read.

- slides that linger (use black slides instead).

Review slides and other support tools, asking yourself:

- Do they keep attention on me—or divert attention away?

- Do they underscore my message—or undermine my message?

- Do they support what I'm saying—or substitute for what I should say?

Ban BULLET POINTS.

At a conference, I sat in on a session entitled "Selling Skills."

The presenter was a successful, creative person who obviously knew his stuff. But I was flabbergasted by his visuals.

He used PowerPoint slides, each bursting at the seams with bullet points. He would read a line on the slide, then comment. Drop to the next line and comment again. And so it went.

His approach was so dismal and cliché, I assumed he was pulling our legs. I figured any minute he would laugh, yell "Got ya!" and tell us this was absolutely the wrong way to deliver presentations.

No such luck. The show went on. And on. Slide after slide after slide. Line after line after line. No photos. No examples. No detours from the crowded bullet points. Before long, napfest.

VISUALS SHOULD SIMPLIFY AND SUPPORT. NOT BURDEN AND BORE.

E.A.S.Y. DOES IT.

Use this acronym's four checkpoints for winning presentations:

ENERGY. When standing before an audience, never go limp and lifeless. Instead, be the audience's main source of energy. And make sure your voice isn't thin or tired. Project.

AWARENESS. Be aware of yourself—stance, voice, gestures. And stay aware of audience members. Are they listening or drifting? Involved or detached? Smiling or scowling? Adjust accordingly.

STRENGTH. Audiences expect you to take charge. Don't overpower, but own the space. Radiate confidence and poise. Be considerate, but direct. Don't stammer or waiver.

YOU. Don't imitate others or hide the real you. Parade your positive traits. Demonstrate your wit and wisdom. Exhibit your passion and compassion. Hold up the very best version of yourself.

Conway's Law.

A NASA engineering team anticipated foam damage well before the disastrous launch of space shuttle Columbia. But when presenting those dangers, the team crammed so many bullet points into its traditional PowerPoint show that their slides were indecipherable.

Which leads us to Conway's Law, a sociological adage named after computer programmer Melvin Conway:

"Organizations are constrained to produce designs that are copies of the communication structures of these organizations."

And my simplified version of Conway's Law as it applies to idea pitches says:

"People and organizations tend to structure new presentations in the same way they've structured previous presentations."

This translation of Conway's Law is often expressed in these kinds of statements:

"We always mount prototypes on boards..."

"I always start by reading the creative brief..."

"We always end with our profile show..."

"We always use kick-ass multimedia..."

"We always use bullet points to help make a logical argument..."

"Dave always does the introduction, then Sarah reviews research..."

DON'T LET PAST PRESENTATIONS—EVEN SUCCESSFUL ONES—DICTATE THE FORMAT FOR THE NEXT PITCH. IT'S A NEW DAY. NEW SITUATION. NEW IDEA.

CHANGE the recipe.

Digital Kitchen creates award-winning film pieces,
motion graphics and interactive work for Nike, Sony,
Budweiser, PBS, Sundance and dozens of other
stellar brands.

But they don't let their multi-media savvy dictate the formats of idea pitches.

"It depends on the client," says Digital Kitchen president
Don McNeill. "Sometimes we'll do polished pieces.
Other times we'll use storyboards. Other times we'll just
explain the visual treatment.

"Or maybe we'll do something totally different—for example, to present a group of PSA spots, we prepared fake
movie posters to show the ideas. The client loved them."

In a word.

Sometimes a slide only needs one word.

One word. Or two. Maybe three. But not a sentence. And, for sure, not a stack of sentences.

For example, if you were discussing the content on page 95 ("Practice Your Pitch"), you might have a slide with:

PRACTICE

or perhaps:

DELIBERATE PRACTICE

or, at most:

STRETCH + FEEDBACK + REPEAT

Just enough words to drive home your main point. Never read sentences off the screen. And don't force your audience to wade through lines of text.

USE WORDS. BUT BE STINGY.

charts and graphs?

Few, if any.

When you show stats, present them in simple ways. Use information design techniques. Be inspired by artists like Nigel Holmes, responsible for many of the clever "snapshot" charts in *USA Today* and *TIME*.

Think of the visual as a magazine ad, suggests speech-writer James Humes. If it's not self-explanatory, forget it.

If you need to explain a slide, you have the wrong slide.

"A WIDE SCREEN JUST MAKES A BAD FILM TWICE AS BAD."

Movie mogul Samuel Goldwyn's famous line also applies to pitches. People often try selling lackluster ideas with visual bells and whistles—but they just make weak ideas look even weaker.

CLICK.

Marketing guru Seth Godin often uses his own snapshots to illustrate messages in his presentations.

Making a case for market differentiation, Godin flashes up snapshots of a mom-and-pop candy store standing out from rows of look-alike franchises on a Canadian highway.

And to underscore the value of being where customers are, Godin's next slide shows an identical candy store built by the same owners on the opposite side of the highway—so they catch customers coming and going.

Fill files with favorite photos that make points and tell stories. Don't worry about polished photography—personal snapshots make presentations more intimate and credible.

MAKE music.

Music composition begins with twelve notes. Literature begins with twenty-six letters. It's not the quantity of resources, but the quality of arrangements and variations.

OUT WITH HANDOUTS.

Handouts are those ubiquitous sets of pages presented before presentations. The intent is for decision makers to follow along as you cover each point.

SPOILER ALERT: PEOPLE FOLLOW HANDOUTS ABOUT AS WELL AS CATS FOLLOW TOUR GUIDES.

They'll jump ahead. Double back. When you're on page one, they're on page six. When you're at page six, they're back at page three. Or they simply speed-read from front to back, then check Blackberries while you listen to yourself talk.

And pray for mercy if you put project costs on the last page. That's the first place they go. They'll run down numbers, shake heads and cluck tongues. Then they'll slide the set aside and stare blankly into space. Goodbye, bright idea.

Hate those handouts.

IN WITH LEAVE-BEHINDS.

Leave-behinds are distributed after the sales pitch. Decision makers review them later. Catch what they miss. Dig deeper into content.

And leave-behinds serve another powerful purpose—decision makers often use them to sell your ideas to their decision makers.

Invest in leave-behinds, not handouts. Make them trenchant and enticing. Succinct, but loaded with samples, photos, examples and case studies—anything to ignite the selling of your ideas.

Ask yourself: If I wanted someone to approve my idea by reviewing this leave-behind—without me whispering in their ear or showing prototypes—what would I include, and how would it look?

Before starting your pitch, let decision makers know that afterward you'll provide comprehensive content. Watch them sit back and stick with you.

Love those leave-behinds.

Feel Books.

As a leave-behind, Reign Agency creates a Feel Book.

"If we want clients to be passionate about an idea, we have to display that same passion," says creative director Stefan Mumaw. "Passion is an emotion, a lengthened discovery of what we believe in."

With that in mind, Reign Agency creates a book of emotions wrapped around the idea. This Feel Book is a blending of fonts, colors, images, styles, sketches, words and graphic treatments.

"This book shows the passion and emotion we infuse in the idea," Mumaw says. "We give the Feel Book to clients at the completion of the presentation. This lets the show continue after the meeting ends."

5. ADD drama.

Enliven presentations with drama. No need to pull out violins and Kleenex, but add theatrics appropriate for you, your audience and your idea.

Maybe a soul-stirring example. A clever story. A propelling fact.

Perhaps a riveting video clip or piece of street theater.

A classic example is when Michael Jager of JDK Design pitched Microsoft on a new identity for Xbox.

He sliced an X in a large sheet of paper and pushed his head through the hole. "X today is all 'AARGGHHH!'" he yelled, like the Incredible Hulk. Then Jager flipped the paper and gracefully moved his hand through it to show how X could become the opening to an experience, one that could transition Xbox from rawness to elegance.

ARE YOU BUILDING EMOTION INTO YOUR PITCHES?

Rollout.

An associate once ended a pitch by unrolling butcher paper on the table in front of clients and passing out crayons. He asked the clients to write or draw how they saw the idea being used by customers.

At first, the clients hesitated. Then one by one, they selected crayons and went to work. Before long, everybody was talking, drawing, laughing—and taking ownership of the idea.

Maybe such theatrics would work for you and your decision makers. Maybe not. But find suitable ways to end your pitch with passion and persuasion.

Don't build up clients only to let them down at the end with "Well, what do you think?" or "That's it."

How many choices?

In talks and seminars, I'm often asked how many options should be presented to decision makers.

It all depends on the idea and client, but I've most often shown one, two or three alternatives—never more than three.

I asked other IdeaSellers the number of choices they prefer presenting:

"Usually two or three."

—David Schimmel, AND PARTNERS

"Depends on the stage of the idea—maybe a half-dozen early in the process, one to three when it's call time."

—Trish Berrong, HALLMARK CARDS

"One to four, depending on the client."

—Don McNeill, DIGITAL KITCHEN

"I show an extremely wide range at the earliest stages, so they can do a little shopping with options. Then, once we lock in on a direction, I blow that focused direction into a bell curve of choices."

—Sally Hogshead, AUTHOR AND COPYWRITER

"Three seems to be the magic number. Something resonates with people's memories of fairy tales when they get three options to choose from—as in, 'This one's juuuuust right.'"

—Lisa Maulhardt, STONE YAMASHITA PARTNERS

ORGANIZING choices.

The follow-up to "How many choices?" is always "In what order should the choices be presented?"

Here's what IdeaSellers said:

"It varies, but usually the best first."
—David Schimmel, AND PARTNERS

"First I show them what they ask for, then the safest, then our preferred recommendation."
—Don McNeill, DIGITAL KITCHEN

"It varies—mostly by how involved the piece is."
—Trish Berrong, HALLMARK CARDS

"I always tell them the order before I start showing so they're not wondering what we're up to. This contributes to the overall honesty of the presentation. I'll say something like, 'We have a set of solutions to show you—we like some more than others, but we're comfortable with everything we'll show.'"
—Jeff Long, DIGITAL KITCHEN

"ONE FOR YOU,
one for me."

In design school, Marcel Wanders initially met rejection from teachers when showing projects.

So he decided to create two versions for every assignment—one version he knew the teacher would like, and another reflecting his own interpretation.

The technique paid off. Wanders won three school design competitions. His final project was featured on the cover of a national design magazine. And before graduation, he had a chair produced by a famous furniture company.

Are decision makers rejecting your favorite ideas? Try Wanders's approach—create one version that satisfies them, and one that thrills you.

"First show them what they want. Then show them what you want them to have."

—Paul Arden, ADVERTISING AND
    FILM CREATIVE DIRECTOR

Tempt.

Look into the eyes of a child reaching for a shiny toy, and into those of a decision maker reaching for an alluring prototype. Not a scintilla of difference.

We're all kids when seeing enticements just out of reach. Want. Want now.

Build on this universal truth when pitching ideas. Don't reveal everything up front. Play the burlesque artist. Tantalize. Tempt. Keep something behind veils.

Presenting a line of luxurious Italian wallets, my product-development team and I walked into the decision maker's office with rolls of raw leather and a polished hardwood box. We unfurled the leather on his desk. He listened to our pitch and asked questions about craft and quality. But he kept glancing toward the box.

After telling stories of how our ideas would delight his customers, we slowly opened the box and held out prototypes.

That look was in his eyes. Sold.

SHOW OFF.

A few years ago, Marcel Wanders presented "The Naked Designer: 10 rules on how to design without fear" to the Industrial Designers Society of America.

He began in a tailored suit, but quickly removed the jacket. With each rule introduced, off came another article of clothing—tie, shirt, belt, shoes. By Rule 9, he was down to his shorts.

For Rule 10, he stepped behind the podium, dropped his shorts and exited the stage wearing a towel.

But then a new slide appeared on the screen: "Rule 11: Always give more than expected."

Wanders, minus towel, streaked from the back, threw candy into the crowd, and—bam!—the auditorium went dark. Wild applause.

NO, YOU DON'T HAVE TO STRIP NAKED, OR EVEN GIVE THE SHIRT OFF YOUR BACK, TO SELL IDEAS. BUT IF YOUR DECISION MAKERS APPRECIATE DRAMA, WHAT CALCULATED RISKS WILL YOU TAKE TO SIZZLE UP THE PITCH?

There's no biz
LIKE SHOW BIZ.

Richard Christiansen, founder of Chandelier Creative, learned the value of showmanship while growing up in Australia. He watched his parents turn their farm into an "Australian experience" for tourists, complete with sheep races, boomerang throwing and a fake tribe of Aborigines.

When Christiansen started his New York agency, an opportunity opened to pitch Nordstrom department stores. But at the time, he only had a meager space and three employees. Not a lot of show for such a giant prospect.

So he called up his theatrical genes and staged an office by renting a large space, furnishing it with flea-market items and hiring a day staff off craigslist.

He got the business and now has lots of name-brand accounts, including Morgans Hotel Group, Liberty of London, Mandarin Oriental Hotel and Old Navy.

And his loft offices include show-biz furnishings such as an amusement-park helicopter, giant Ronald McDonald head, latex sofa and purple piano.

SHAMAN
ON SHOWMANSHIP.

Marc English has been called a "teacher, preacher, shaman and showman." For his rollicking and popular talks to designers and other groups, English shows up in mariachi outfits, Scottish kilts and white linen suits. Each speech begins with live music and ends with his ritual tossing of glitter.

But when it comes to idea pitches, the Austin-based designer makes sure any showmanship matches the personalities and tastes of decision makers.

"A lecture has me front and center," he says, "but client meetings, by their very nature, are not about me."

If, however, the client is open to sizzle, English, who authored *Designing Identity*, uses showmanship to help make points about his concepts.

"We were presenting to a new client in New York that I knew was left-of-center," he says. "It was winter, so I arrived wearing a thick wool sweater. During the presentation, I slowly unzipped and removed the sweater, revealing a western shirt covered in silver rhinestones, embroidery and white fringe.

"The shirt was over the top, but I was using it to make a point about identity, perception and reality. The antics broke the ice, got lots of laughs and let the client know I understood identity on both personal and professional levels."

Playing it straight.

Although English is known for costumes and clowning on the lecture circuit, he often leaves theatrics at home when meeting with clients.

"In client pitches, I have on occasion used sound bites from my lectures," he says. "But in most cases, I don't think clients want either theatrics or a show.

"They want to be listened to and reassured they've hired someone who takes the time to understand them. Any words or theatrics carried over from my lectures have to underscore that I take clients seriously and that we can work together.

"If you choose to use theatrics in client presentations, my advice is to make it personal, make it memorable and leave with a laugh, often at your own expense.

"The only place for jaw-dropping is in the work, not the words."

ABRACADABRA
moments.

Remember when Steve Jobs introduced the incredibly thin MacBook Air by sliding it from a manila envelope? Truly an abracadabra moment—as magical as a rabbit pulled from a hat.

Look for ways to create dramatic, abracadabra moments in your presentations. It has to be appropriate for the idea and the decision maker—otherwise, you'll slip into silliness. But when it works, it's spellbinding.

We were reviewing home-office products when a supplier opened his briefcase and dumped out its contents—notes, receipts, bills, paper clips, pads, pens, business cards. He then pulled out a leather organizer and, in less than two minutes, placed everything in its proper place.

SOLD.

Stroke of GENIUS.

To present concepts for his Chicago Spire tower, architect Santiago Calatrava strolled to an overhead projector and opened a box of watercolors.

He sketched a slender, vertical leaf and a snail's shell, inspirations for his building, which has the slogan of "Inspired by nature, imagined by Calatrava."

When seven architects presented at a competition to design a train station, six showed up with large teams and huge stacks of past work. Calatrava appeared with his watercolors and left with the commission.

And to introduce his idea for a transit hub at the World Trade Center site, Calatrava drew a child releasing a bird. The sketch poetically conveyed his concept of glass-and-steel canopies arching like outstretched wings.

COULD YOUR IDEA BE PRESENTED WITH A QUICK SKETCH? A DRAMATIC PHOTO? A POETIC VERSE? A SINGLE WORD?

HOLE-IN-ONE.

After James Cameron directed *The Terminator*, he arranged a meeting with studio heads to discuss his next project.

Cameron wanted to pitch a sequel to *Alien*, although he had not directed the original film. It was a hard sell, because *Alien* was "not a massive financial success," according to film producer Gordon Carroll, who attended the presentation.

Cameron walked into the room empty-handed—no slides, handouts or notes.

Instead, he went to the chalkboard and wrote the word "ALIEN."

Then he added an *S* to make it "ALIENS." Then he drew a vertical line through the *S* to make it "ALIEN$."

He turned to his decision makers and smiled. And that day he received $18-million advance for the film.

HOLE-IN-ONE PITCHES
need perfect conditions.

Opportunities like Calatrava's and Cameron's are rare. But if the right idea is presented by the right person to the right audience, a hole-in-one approach can work.

Proceed if you have the perfect storm for this calculated risk:

1. DECISION MAKERS WHO APPRECIATE DRAMA.
Cameron presented to the right audience for his theatrics—Hollywood execs who live and breathe show business.

2. KNOWLEDGE OF WANTS, NEEDS, HOPES AND FEARS.
Cameron knew decision makers were fretting over whether or not an *Alien* sequel could make money.

3. CREDIBILITY OF PRESENTER.
Cameron was the right person to make this type of pitch. He was a young, respected director with a proven ability to make successful films. He had just directed the profitable *Terminator*.

MY GODSON

is a *selling superboy.*

At a family reunion, my six-year-old godson, Thomas, converted thirty dollars into a hundred in less than an hour.

He began by asking if I had any large bills he could see. I showed him a fifty.

"Will you take thirty dollars for it?" Thomas asked.

"No, but if you'll save until you have forty dollars," I said, "you'll have a deal."

So he walked over to his Uncle Joe and sold him two crayon drawings for ten dollars. A few minutes later, he collected my fifty.

Then he went to his Uncle Bruce and asked if he had any large bills. Bruce let him hold a hundred.

Thomas: "Would you take a fifty for it?"

Bruce: "No."

Thomas: "Will you take seventy-five?"

Bruce: "Yes."

Thomas negotiated with his father for a fifteen-dollar advance on his allowance. He arranged to do chores for two aunts for five dollars each, paid in advance.

He took his loot to Uncle Bruce, and within seconds he pocketed a crisp hundred-dollar bill.

SIX LESSONS

FROM A SIX-YEAR-OLD.

Lessons from Thomas's reunion success story:

1. KNOW YOUR DECISION MAKERS.

Thomas knew the easy hits in the family and how to approach each of us.

2. PAY ATTENTION TO DETAILS.

Something tells me Thomas already knew which bills I had after watching me pay for lunch.

3. ASK FOR WHAT YOU WANT.

No problem for Thomas!

4. PICK YOUR TIMING.

He sensed the reunion was a festive, giving occasion. And he was careful not to approach us during adult talk.

5. BE WILLING TO COMPROMISE.

"You won't take thirty—OK, how about forty?"

6. BE APPRECIATIVE.

Thomas sincerely thanked me when I gave him the fifty, and a few days later, he sent a hand-drawn thank-you card. Priceless.

ONCE YOU'VE SOLD SOMETHING,
don't buy it back.

I worked with a designer who was one of the best at pitching ideas. Mike was smart, articulate and passionate. But he didn't know when to sit down.

Clients could whistle, cheer and practically wave currency in his face, but Mike never let that stop him. He kept right on talking—and the more he talked, the more those clients began to reconsider.

After a few painful we-had-'em-then-lost-'em episodes, Mike finally learned to quit when ahead. He grasped the notion of leaving the audience begging for more rather than begging for mercy.

"When you've sold the idea, stop," says Don McNeill of Digital Kitchen. "I can't tell you how many times I've heard creative people go on and on. And eventually the process starts all over again."

IF THEY SAY YES,

BOLT.

"I have watched parades of creative people destroy their own work—after the client finally buys into their ideas," says Brian Collins of COLLINS:.

"They blab themselves right out of a client's approval," he says. "They start to explain the subtle nuances of their solution and compliment the client for their vision. This really pisses people off.

"For goodness sake, if they finally say yes, then say thank you and leave the room with your idea sold. Tell them you will pick up the conversation later or call on the phone or send an e-mail or drop a telegram.

"BUT WHATEVER YOU DO, BOLT."

WRAP IT UP!

I once accepted a request to give a pro bono talk at a local senior center.

I was enthusiastic about the topic, "Creatively Living Your Entire Life." But sixty seconds into my talk, a woman in the audience yelled, "Wrap it up!"

I smiled nervously and kept rolling. But two minute later, she again shouted "Wrap it up!" Lordy, lordy. I hasten the pace even more, skipping a hunk of my content. Only after the third "Wrap it up!" in under five minutes did the center's coordinator slip me a note:

"Sorry—forgot to warn you about old Martha. She has dementia and yells at all our speakers. Don't mind her."

Ladies sitting next to Martha eventually piped her down with loving shhhhs and soft pats. But you better believe I was still determined to wrap it up.

Ever since, when I catch myself getting long-winded or see people checking watches, I'll hear Martha screaming, "Wrap it up!"

WRAP UP. ASK UP.
Listen up.

WRAP UP.
When you've finished your pitch, summarize. Move into options and next steps.

ASK UP.
Assume the sale by asking a question, such as:

"What do you see as the next step?"

"Which of these do you see as the best option?

"When do you think we can we get moving on this?"

LISTEN UP.
Be quiet and wait for the decision maker to speak. If there's a pause, resist the urge to fill the void. Stay silent and listen. You're about to hear something important. Maybe you'll get the go-ahead. Or you'll hear the objection or obstacle you must address to gain approvals.

7

HOW TO HANDLE
OBJECTIONS.

"I take rejection as someone blowing a bugle
in my ear to wake me up and get going, rather
than retreat."

—Sylvester Stallone, ACTOR

<u>OBJECTIONS</u>
are *good* things.

Your decision makers don't say a word during your entire presentation. Uh oh. It's rarely because they are mesmerized by your words. More likely, they've lost interest and are thinking about lunch.

So if you get objections, don't despair. Your decision makers are paying attention. And if you'll read between their lines, you'll gain insights.

You hear objections, but behind the words they may be thinking:

"I'm interested in your idea, but you haven't fully sold me yet."

or

"I want to test you out—let's see how committed you really are to this idea."

or

"I love the overall concept, but it needs tweaking for my approval."

or

"I'm sold, but now I have to sell my boss. Here's the objection she'll have."

Even if decision makers have daunting objections, it's best they be aired during the presentation.

THE WORST SCENARIO IS WALKING AWAY WITH THE IDEA STILL IN YOUR HANDS AND THE OBJECTIONS STILL IN THEIR MINDS.

CHECK
your reactions.

When objections are aired during a pitch, we often:

recoil **CRINGE** TENSE up

deflate **BECOME ANGRY** *respond quickly*

answer tersely. PLUNGE to the next point

*GET THE HELL **OUT OF THERE***

Examine these reactions in daylight. Will they overcome objections and sell ideas?

Nope. They'll likely send your ideas straight to the scrap pile.

Rather than negatively reacting, train yourself to positively respond by:

1. RELAXING
2. LISTENING
3. PAUSING
4. AGREEING
5. ASKING

PAUSE. AGREE. ASK.

PAUSE.
After an objection, allow yourself a few seconds to decide how to respond.

AGREE.
Acknowledge the decision maker's concern and agree with feelings behind it: "I understand why you would feel that way..." or "I can appreciate your concern..." or "I can see why you would want to stop me on that point..."

ASK.
Clarify the decision maker's objection by stating it as a question: "When you say you don't like the artwork, can you tell me more about the problems you see?" or "When you say this doesn't fit your strategy, can you help me see where it departs?" or "I understand why you might think this project looks risky, but will you elaborate on where we could meet trouble?"

"Every sale has five basic obstacles: no need, no money, no hurry, no desire, no trust."

—Zig Ziglar, SALES EXPERT

HEAR OBJECTIONS
as questions.

Brian Tracy, author and sales guru, says the best way to receive an objection is by converting it into a question in your head.

IF YOUR DECISION MAKER SAYS:
"I don't like the copy you've written."

IN YOUR MIND, HEAR HIM SAYING:
"Will you help me understand how your copy works for our audience?"

OR IF THE DECISION MAKER SAYS:
"I'm not crazy about this artwork."

HEAR HER SAYING:
"Will you help me see why you created this artwork to solve our problem?"

OR IF THE DECISION MAKER SAYS:
"This concept is totally off strategy."

HEAR HER SAYING:
"Will you help me connect your concept to our strategy?"

This approach immediately:

- HELPS REMOVE THE OBJECTION'S SHARP EDGES

- HELPS YOU RELAX AND NOT BECOME DEFENSIVE

- HELPS YOU POSITION YOURSELF AS AN ADVISER

PREPARE

FOR OBJECTIONS.

Never lull yourself into assuming there'll be no objections.

OPTIMISM IS FINE, BUT UNPREPARED IS FOOLISH.

Missiles of objection will be fired. The bigger the idea, the larger the attack. You're asking decision makers to let go of something familiar and embrace something new. That means pushback. Lots of it.

Before presenting, take a sheet of paper and create the missile defense form shown on the next page.

Under Missile, list every objection you can imagine. Include the predictable, but also the outlandish. Imagine hard ques-

tions. Relentless questions. Ridiculous questions. Involve team members. Show the idea to family, friends, co-workers, strangers. Solicit their concerns. Add pages as necessary.

Then begin the real work. Under Defense, articulate your response to each objection. Carefully craft your answers.

Don't stop until you have solid replies for every objection. And if you can't develop a response? Back to the drawing board to refine the idea.

Will every possible missile be fired during the pitch? Unlikely. But you'll be ready for what comes your way. And you'll deliver a stronger, confident presentation.

MISSILE *defense system.*

Here's the tool discussed on the preceding page. Create this form on a sheet of paper and use when preparing IdeaSelling presentations.

MISSILE DEFENSE SYSTEM

IDEA:

Missile	Defense

Disarming
OBJECTIONS.

Try answering some objections while you're presenting—before the objections are voiced by decision makers. You'll reduce their sting and add substance to your pitch. For example:

ANTICIPATED OBJECTION:
Decision maker will worry about how employees will react to the idea.

DISARMING THE OBJECTION:
"You may be concerned about how employees will feel about this idea. Our team also had that concern. That's why we've outlined an internal campaign to help explain the concept to employees..."

ANTICIPATED OBJECTION:
Ideas for the brochure's photography will be perceived by decision makers as too expensive.

DISARMING THE OBJECTION:
"The photography won't be inexpensive, as I'm sure you know. But these captivating photos can give the brochure the appearance of a high-end magazine. Prospects will keep the piece on their desks and show it to others. And we can extend our dollars by producing high-quality prints and providing these as gifts to prospects and customers..."

ANTICIPATED OBJECTION:
Implementing will take more time than the decision maker will want to allocate.

DISARMING THE OBJECTION:
"This campaign will likely take a few weeks longer than previous ones, but I'll offer three reasons why it's worth the extra time. I'll also show ways we can implement the campaign in stages to immediately realize benefits..."

PICK YOUR battles.

Nobody likes dealing with someone who rolls out a nuclear arsenal to defend every detail.

Suggest a comma might be unnecessary, and it's World War Three. Mention a photo could be shot from a different angle and get ready to duel. Question the reason for a particular budget item, and, well, them's fightin' words.

If you're that type of presenter, chill. Don't waste energy and blow goodwill. Life's too short.

Instead, know the tipping points of your idea—places where large or small changes would spark significantly different results.

Fight for these critical tipping points. Graciously concede or compromise on less-important items.

You'll be viewed as flexible and accommodating. And these small concessions will help you gather goodwill to spend on true tipping points.

zugzwang.

Zugzwang is a state of play in chess where any move open to the player will damage his position. If during a meeting with decision makers you find yourself in a zugzwang situation—a damned-if-you-do, damned-if-you-don't situation—look for an exit. Return to play another day.

CLING TO
what counts.

What are the main tipping points of your idea—
those areas where changes would spark significantly
different results?

1.
2.
3.
4.
5.

Find ways to earn approvals for these critical points.

COMPROMISE OR CONCEDE ON
LESS-IMPORTANT DETAILS.

Sugarcoatings.

Sometimes you need to prepare decision makers for your next thought or signal you're about to switch gears in your approach. Sugarcoatings can save the day.

If you need to critique an existing idea that's a favorite of the decision maker, your sugarcoating might be:

"Steve, I've wrestled with how to say what I'm about to say, because I understand how important this is to you..."

Such a line doesn't alter the decision maker's views, of course, but it coats your delivery and glides him along.

Or maybe you need to introduce research backing your idea but bashing one of the client's business practices. Your sugarcoating could be:

"I'm about to give the only piece of bad news you'll hear from me today..."

This doesn't convert bad news to good. But it helps the client mentally brace herself and shows you empathize with her feelings. And it reassures her that your overall presentation will soon continue on a positive track.

Perhaps you simply want decision makers to listen while you give an example. Your sugarcoating might be:

"Let me ask you to sit back and relax while I tell a two-minute story that underscores why I'm here today..."

This helps decision makers rearrange their minds and shows you're respectful of their time. You're telling them not to worry, that the presentation isn't drifting off into a salmagundi of rambling tales.

Create YOUR SUGARCOATINGS.

Prepare three sugarcoatings appropriate for your decision makers.

SUGARCOATING TO USE WHEN CRITIQUING AN EXISTING IDEA:

SUGARCOATING TO USE WHEN DELIVERING BAD NEWS:

SUGARCOATING TO USE BEFORE A STORY OR EXAMPLE:

Straight talk.

Honesty is the proverbial best policy in presentations. And, as mentioned on preceding pages, such truthfulness should usually be delivered with diplomatic and emollient sugarcoating.

At times, however, a response to an objection needs to be straightforward. Considerate but straight talk.

With practice, you'll know when to deliver this type of response. It's usually when there are no clear objections; the person is just unwilling to make decisions.

After hemming and hawing, he probably says something like: "Well, let me think about this for a week or so, and I'll get back with you."

Your straight response: "Adam, I understand this is a big decision. (Pause) But if you need to think about it, then I haven't done a good job explaining why it's a valuable idea. What's your main concern with what I've presented today?"

He'll either express a concern or admit he has no real issues.

YOUR STRAIGHT TALK WILL HARD-ELBOW HIM INTO ACTION.

GUT HONEST.

Gut honesty sometimes helps sell ideas.

When Donald Keough was Coca-Cola's president, his team presented a plan requiring a huge investment in eastern Europe. Keough killed the idea.

After the meeting, the head of international operations came into Keough's office. He asked Keough to rethink his decision. Keough had not recently been to eastern Europe, the man stressed, so he didn't appreciate the changes happening there.

Keough listened. He eventually agreed to travel the region and see for himself. Three months later, he approved a billion-dollar investment in eastern Europe.

"If that man hadn't had the guts to come into my office and tell me how stupid I was being," Keough told *The New York Times*, "we wouldn't have the kind of business we have there now."

GUIDELINES

for GUT HONESTY.

You'll know when you need to be gut honest with a client
or boss about a rejected idea. When that time comes:

1. Be discreet—meet privately with the person.

*2. Be respectful—say what you mean,
   but don't say it mean.*

3. Be direct—keep it concise and focused.

4. Be credible—stick to the facts.

*5. Be positive—point out the problem, then
   offer a solution.*

"Stop wearing your wishbone
where your backbone ought to be."
—Elizabeth Gilbert, WRITER

KNOW *no.*

KNOW NO WHEN FACING A CONDITION.
If the decision maker has a $5,000 budget, and you have a $50,000 idea, her no expresses a condition, not an objection. Accept the no and come back with a workable solution.

KNOW NO WHEN YOU DON'T KNOW.
When asked for answers you don't have, say no. Return with answers in a reasonable time.

KNOW NO WHEN YOU CAN'T DELIVER.
Say no when you can't meet requests. Explain why and suggest options.

"It's OK to sometimes say 'no' or 'I don't know,'" says Jeff Long of Digital Kitchen. "Creative people get into the most trouble by promising what they can't deliver or by trying to give an answer when they don't have one."

IF YOU'RE KNOCKED DOWN,
go back to basics.

You may remember figure skating's horrific accident at the 2004 Skate America competition involving Tatiana Totmianina and Maxim Marinin. Totmianina fell from Marinin's overhead lift and crashed headfirst into the ice.

She physically recovered, but regaining confidence was difficult for both her and Marinin. As a solution, their coach had them go back to basics. In slow motion, they performed successful routines from when they first started skating together.

The process worked. Totmianina and Marinin returned to win an Olympics gold medal in 2006.

Has your idea been knocked down? If so, go back to basics. Recall a time you sold an idea, when you knocked it out of the park. Replay the details in slow motion. Feel success.

Perhaps you'll see a better way to present the idea. Maybe you'll discover a detail you forgot to include. Recalling past success—as was done by Totmianina and Marinin—will restore confidence and help you suit up for another day.

RESCUE MISSION.

When chef David Chang first conceived Ssäm Bar in Manhattan, he envisioned a lunch spot featuring gourmet "fast foods." But his location on lower 2nd Avenue turned out to be wrong for the concept—not enough offices to generate lunch crowds for an upscale menu.

So did Chang abandon his idea? Did he curse fate and shut down the joint?

No, he adjusted. Chang made Ssäm Bar a late-night destination, open from 10:30 PM to 2:30 AM These hours attracted the after-party crowd as well as chefs who drifted in after finishing up at their own restaurants.

The chefs loved Chang's dishes. They spread the word. Chang soon became part of their club and a successful, respected restaurant owner.

WHEN YOUR IDEAS HIT WALLS, ADJUST. REARRANGE TO ATTRACT DIFFERENT MARKETS. RECONFIGURE TO HANDLE OBJECTIONS. REFOCUS TO MEET REALITIES.

Rescue the mission.

Observe *and adjust,*

Brian Collins, chief creative officer at COLLINS:, tells of being invited to pitch a tech firm that claimed in phone conversations to be "open, passionate and innovative."

But when Collins arrived at their headquarters, he was ushered into a dark, windowless conference room. "One decision maker refused to look up from his laptop and the others were talking among themselves," says Collins. "The senior decision maker took the traditional power seat far away from her staff.

"I knew right then my presentation for their 'open, passionate and innovative' culture was all wrong. I was facing an old-school, closed, hierarchical culture."

But Collins plowed ahead. "And it was awful," he says. "Epically awful. Would not have been more awful had I jumped on the conference table and performed Riverdance in a red Speedo and flip-flops.

"If I had only taken a few minutes to step outside and reframe the dialogue with input received from their environment, I would have dumped the presentation and just talked with them.

"They truly wanted help and knew they needed change. And we could have provided good solutions. But I didn't start the right conversation, and they went with someone else.

"Next time, I'll listen better. Even to the furniture."

Believe
AND BUILD.

"You have to believe in what you're doing," says Jakob Trollbäck of Trollbäck + Company. "People are going to take shots, even at great ideas."

He remembers Richard Saul Wurman, TED Conference founder, saying, "Don't bother to criticize anything that doesn't attempt to be brilliant."

Keep believing in your idea as you learn from the criticism, Trollbäck suggests. And look for ways to build on the idea. "If we have an idea the client doesn't buy, we may go back to them on another pitch and say, 'Remember that idea we showed you before? Maybe it would work here...'"

"Truth crushed to the earth shall rise again."
—Dr. Martin Luther King, Jr.

SAYING *you're sorry.*

There was the time my storyboards knocked a water pitcher into the laps of decision makers. The time I used indelible markers on the client's shiny new whiteboards. The time I called a client by his dog's name. And those dreadful times early in my career when I naively promised more than I could deliver.

If we make enough pitches, we'll make mistakes. "Holy cow, where to begin?" says copywriter Sally Hogshead. "I'd say forgetting the portfolio for a client pitch ranks right up there."

SO WHAT TO DO WHEN YOU SCREW UP? START BY SAYING YOU'RE SORRY.

"You'll need to rebuild trust and cooperation to repair the relationship," says Maurice Schweitzer, a Wharton School professor. "One obvious yet powerful tool for doing so is an apology."

HOME RUN

OR RUN HOME.

Apologies and selling situations are a lot like baseball stars and steroids, says Dave Kurlan, sales adviser.

Baseball players who promptly admitted steroid use and apologized quickly fell out of the news. On the other hand, players who denied or delayed seemed forever in the spotlight.

Recall the practices of those baseball players when debating whether or not to make apologies in selling situations, Kurlan suggests.

"If a customer attacks, complains, whines, demands or points fingers, and you simply say, 'You're right, I'm sorry,' the issue goes away," he says. "However, if you get defensive, place blame, make excuses, deny the issue or fail to apologize, your customer will never forget and, as a result, may no longer be your customer."

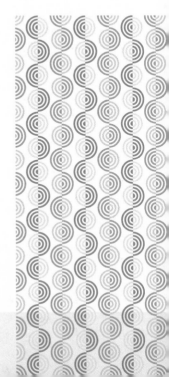

SEVEN WAYS
to apologize.

Sooner or later, we'll inadvertently piss off decision makers. Sincere apologies start the process of repairing damages.

Maurice Schweitzer and two fellow professors at Wharton School studied apology-making and identified seven components of an apology:

1. STATEMENT: "I'm sorry."

2. EXPRESSION OF REMORSE: "I feel really bad about this."

3. SELF-CASTIGATION: "I can't believe I said that."

4. OFFER TO REPAIR: "What can I do to make things right?"

5. REQUEST FOR FORGIVENESS: "What I did was wrong. Please forgive me."

6. PROMISE REGARDING FUTURE BEHAVIOR: "I promise to be more careful."

7. EXPLANATION: "I should have personally checked that. It won't happen again."

Effective apologies include some or all components, according to Schweitzer. Whopper mistakes call for all seven.

Always be sincere. "If the recipient thinks your apology is less than sincere," says Schweitzer, "she is unlikely to forgive you. Convey sincerity by delivering the apology in person, expressing it with emotion and conveying a sense of personal responsibility and remorse."

8

AND THEN IT'S
FOLLOW-UP
and more.

"Those who are blessed with the most talent
don't necessarily outperform everyone else.
It's the people with follow-through who excel."
—Mary Kay Ash, BUSINESS LEADER

FOLLOW UP.

My wife is the best salesperson I know.

Throughout her career, Hope has hit top sales numbers every time—with medical devices, real estate, artwork, you name it. She's had this selling gene since childhood, her mother tells me, first displaying it by being the best hawker of Girl Scout cookies Fort Lauderdale has ever seen.

In truth, she can't quit selling, even when it's not her product. We'll be in a cookware store and next thing I know, she's vanished. I'll find her in the next aisle, explaining to a shopper why one espresso machine is better than the others. "You don't work here," I'll remind her.

Hope tells me the real secret to her success is follow-up. And I've seen her practice what she preaches over and over. After a presentation or sales call, she works on action steps from the meeting. She also sends thank-you notes or treats. She returns phone calls and e-mails before sundown. And if a client has a snag or problem, she's on it.

"Follow-ups let clients know you care, but about 90 percent of salespeople don't seem to do it," she says.

"SO BY SIMPLY RETURNING MESSAGES AND FOLLOWING THROUGH ON DETAILS, YOU PLACE YOURSELF IN THE TOP 10 PERCENT."

FOLLOW-UP *tips.*

1. LET THE CLIENT KNOW HOW YOU'LL FOLLOW UP.

Before leaving the meeting, review what happens next. If the idea was accepted, discuss implementation steps. If the idea was rejected or needs revisions, suggest next steps and time frames.

2. MAKE POST-MEETING NOTES.

Back at your workspace, immediately review the meeting on paper. Use the presentation review shown on the following page or devise your own technique.

3. DOWNLOAD WITH YOUR TEAM.

Hold a brief download session—talk about what went right, what went wrong, decision-maker reactions, lessons learned, tips for next time and action steps.

4. PAUSE BEFORE ACTING.

Take a break before making decisions or jumping into action. Give your mind time to calm down and adjust, especially if the meeting didn't fit your expectations. Things always appear differently after lunch or the next day.

5. SEND THANK-YOU NOTES.

For outside clients or prospects, consider handwritten notes. For internal clients, e-mails can do the job. Keep these short and sweet, thanking decision makers for their time and feedback.

6. SEND A SUMMARY.

Within forty-eight hours, provide decision makers with a concise, written summary of the meeting, action steps and any timetables.

PRESENTATION *review.*

DATE:

LOCATION:

IDEA AND/OR MEETING TOPIC:

ATTENDEES:

SHORT SUMMARY:

QUESTIONS I WAS ASKED:

OBJECTIONS RAISED:

INSIGHTS:

NEXT STEPS:

THE ART OF
saying *thank you.*

For years, I was associated with singer John Denver and his environmental projects. I always admired the way he connected with people.

Whenever someone gave him a compliment, whether on the street or backstage, he would pause, look directly at the person and simply say "thank you."

Not "glad you liked it," or "thanks," or "happy to hear it." And certainly no deflections such as "I wish the sound system had been better." No, he would look people right in their eyes and sincerely say "thank you."

Then came something interesting. John would redirect attention to the other person by asking him or her a question, like "Where are you from?" or "What types of music do you like?" or "What are your environmental concerns?"

It worked every time. For those few minutes, that person felt special and connected with the person they took time to compliment.

The next time you receive a compliment during or after a pitch, try this approach.

> *Look the person in the eyes and sincerely say "thank you." Then ask a question that returns attention to the other person.*

FOR WRITERS *only.*

For various reasons—some valid, some vain—copy often passes through endless chains of approvals. Executives, lawyers and accountants suddenly become copy-editors and grammar teachers.

As a result, writers often suffer the death of a thousand cuts. Here are a few tips for making the copy-approval process easier:

1. STOP CALLING IT AN APPROVAL PROCESS. Don't ask for approval, ask for input. Ask reviewers to only check for accuracy of facts and figures.

2. DELIVER TECHNICALLY PERFECT COPY. Double-check—no, triple-check—grammar, punctuation and spelling. Flawless copy earns less scrutiny. Copy with a misspelled word or misplaced comma instantly loses credibility and invites close inspection and heavy editing.

3. CUT THE NUMBER OF EYES. The more the messier when it comes to reviewing copy. Talk with your manager or client about the pitfalls of committee edits and trim the routing list.

4. DISTRIBUTE HARD COPIES OR PDFS. If you distribute Word documents by e-mail, brace yourself for cuts, pastes and rewrites—you've made it far too easy to edit. Send hard copies, and single-space to make the pieces more tamper-resistant.

5. INCLUDE AN INSTRUCTIONAL COVER SHEET. Explain how to provide feedback and what should be reviewed. Provide a deadline, adding: "If we have not received your feedback by this date, we'll assume you found no inaccuracies."

6. ESTABLISH A TRACK RECORD. Nothing bypasses editing like showing you're the expert. Meet objectives and communicate in a compelling, creative way. Prove your pieces hit the mark, and you'll stop target practice.

PERSISTENCE.

When The Gates unfurled in New York City, the art project created a visual golden river in Central Park. For two weeks, more than 7,000 "gates" with free-hanging saffron fabric lined the park's twenty-three miles of footpaths and walkways.

Environmental artists Christo and Jeanne-Claude first developed the concept for The Gates in 1979, but met roadblocks and pushback for the next twenty-five years. They would present to a city council and receive approvals, then a mayor would veto it. Or they would get a mayor to agree, only to have a parks commissioner nix it.

But the two artists never gave up. They would step back, rework their presentations and try again. "We never changed an idea," said Jeanne-Claude. "We only crystallized it and made it clearer."

Because of their massive scale, all of the pair's projects involved years of contentious meetings with town councils, property owners and environmental regulators. But Christo and Jeanne-Claude viewed such presentations as part of the artistic process, convinced the back-and-forth added creative force.

"A THOUSAND PEOPLE TRY TO HELP US," SAID JEANNE-CLAUDE, "AND A THOUSAND PEOPLE TRY TO STOP US. THIS CREATES ENERGY."

"If they take away my paints, I'll use watercolors. If they take those away, I'll use pencils and if they take those away, I'll use crayons. And if they strip me naked and throw me in a cell, I'll spit on my finger and draw on the wall."

—Pablo Picasso

KEEP *playing.*

Acclaimed type designer Matthew Carter first studied type in London. He then moved to New York City, but was intimidated by the quality and variety of design. He pondered giving up and moving back to London.

But one evening he ventured into a jazz club where the John Coltrane Quartet was performing. He was astonished by the group's talent and returned to hear them many times.

"Sometimes they played the same songs in the second set as they played in the first," Carter told *The New Yorker.* "Not because they were lazy, but because they wanted to surpass themselves or find something in the music that they hadn't found earlier in the evening."

Carter decided to persist in New York. "The group's seriousness of purpose was a lesson," said Carter. "I could have been dishonest enough to return to England and say I hadn't seen great design. But I couldn't somehow pretend that I hadn't heard the John Coltrane Quartet."

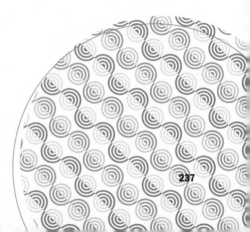

PLANT A POTATO,
get a potato.

We reap what we sow.

Display distrust and distrust comes back.

Tense up and the room fills with tension.

Act somber and grim faces stare back.

Relax and tensions melt.

Show trust and earn trust.

Flash a smile and everyone lights up.

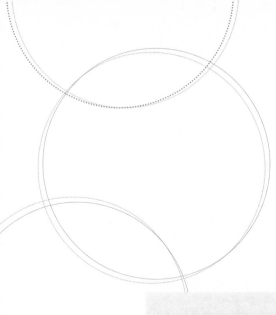

"You haven't learned life's lesson very well if you haven't noticed that you can give the tone or color, or decide the reaction you want of people in advance. It's unbelievably simple. If you want them to take an interest in you, take an interest in them first. If you want to make them nervous, become nervous yourself. It's as simple as that. People will treat you as you treat them. It's no secret. Look about you. You can prove it with the next person you meet."

—Sir Winston Churchill

YOU NEVER AGAIN HAVE TO SAY
"They just don't get it."

I started this book saying it's not enough to have ideas—that we also have to sell those ideas. I said moaning about how clients "just don't get it" won't bring ideas to life—ideas come to life when presentations come to life.

Those things were said on page 1. So unless you've skipped 200-plus pages between then and now, you're reading this as a different person.

You're no longer a victim saying "they don't get it."

No longer winging pitches or fretting over objections.

No longer lacking confidence, composure and credibility.

In other words, you're an IdeaSeller.

But don't stop now.

Continue to work the exercises. Watch others present. Ask questions. Listen. Practice, practice, practice. Test the efficacy of what you've discovered in upcoming pitches. Own what works. Put aside the rest.

And when you sell an idea, celebrate. Pat your back. Congratulate team members. Maybe e-mail me at sdh@mindspring. com to say: "You know those decision makers that didn't get it? Well, this time they got it."

HAPPY PITCHING,
Sam

acknowledgments.

My deepest gratitude to the highly creative people and IdeaSellers included in this book. Your insights and generosity made this book possible.

Special thanks to these talented individuals who went above and beyond as an informal panel, providing advice and comments: Cathy Austin, Loop9 Marketing; Trish Berrong, Hallmark Cards; Brian Collins, COLLINS:; Marc English, Marc English Design; Sally Hogshead, author, speaker and copywriter; Jeff Long and Don McNeill, Digital Kitchen; Lisa Maulhardt, Stone Yamashita Partners; Stefan Mumaw, Reign Agency; Al Ries, Ries & Ries; David Schimmel, And Partners; DJ Stout, Pentagram; and Jakob Trollbäck, Trollbäck + Company.

Warm appreciation to my editor, Amy Schell Owen, and designer, Grace Ring, for providing their counsel and skills in bringing the book to life, and to Megan Patrick at HOW Books, who first collaborated with me on the concept. And to all the other outstanding people at *HOW* magazine and conferences for their support and friendship.

To the clients, associates and teams I've worked with over the years, thank you for helping me become an IdeaSeller.

Thank you to those who attend my talks and seminars, for your energy and participation. And to my students at Portfolio Center, for keeping me on my toes.

In memory of my brother Phil, who taught me so much about selling, writing, creativity and living. And in honor of my brother Bruce and sister, Diana, who continue to love, teach and support me and many others.

AND MOST OF ALL, TO HOPE.

end notes

18   *Win the Crowd*, Steve Cohen, HarperCollins Publishers, Inc., 2005

21   *Nothing in Common*, Delphi Films, 1986

24   *Emotions of Normal People*, Dr. William Moulton Marston, Cooper Press, 2008; Integrative Psychology—Study of Unit, Dr. William Moulton Marston, Iyer Press, 3/07; http://en.wikipedia.org/wiki/DISC_assessment

30   "How to Sell a Mustang," Ben Stein, *The New York Times*, 9/25/05

31   "Brothers sell lobsterman experience along with catch," Clarke Canfield, AP. *USA Today*, 12/10/07; "You're the Lobsterman," *Down East*, 3/08

33   "Why QVC Is Sold on the Internet," Paul C. Judge, *Fast Company*, 2/01

36   The Mind of the Negotiator, Deepak Malhotra and Max H. Bazerman, Harvard Business School, articles in Negotiation Newsletter, 8/07

45   http://sethgodin.typepad.com/seths_blog/2008/09/time.html

54   "Source Credibility Dimensions in Marketing Communications—A Generalized Solution," Martin Eisend, Freie Universitat Berlin, Journal of the Empirical Generalisations in Marketing, 2006; "Components of Credibility of a Favorable News Source," Michael W. Singletary, Journalism Quarterly, 53; "It's Not What You Say, It's how You Say It," James P.T. Fatt, *Communication World*, 6/99

57   "Renzo Piano's Expansion of the Morgan Library Transforms a World of Robert Barons and Scholars," Nicolai Ouroussoff, *The New York Times*, 4/1/06

60   "Confidence Game," Drake Bennett, 8/17/08, *Boston Globe*, www.boston.com

64   *USA Today*, 3/21/08

68   "A Higher Calling," Lynn Hirschberg, *New York Times Magazine*, 12/21/08

71   Seth's Blog, 3/4/09, http://sethgodin.typepad.com/seths_blog

85   "It's not what you say, it's how you say it," James P.T. Fatt, *Communication World*, 6/99; www.stevenaitchison.co.uk/blog, 8/11/07

87   "Pupils must look away to think," BBC News, 1/11/06

90   "A Higher Calling," Lynn Hirschberg, *New York Times Magazine*, 12/21/08

92   *Every Second Counts*, Lance Armstrong with Sally Jenkins, Broadway Publishing, 2003

93   "What it takes to be great," Geoffrey Colvin, *Fortune* 10/19/06

99   "Confessions of a TED Addict," Virginia Heffernan, *New York Times Magazine*, 1/25/09

101	*The Power of Design*, Greenway Communications, 2008. TEDxAtlanta Event, September 15, 2009.
117	"Phelps feared he wouldn't be strong enough to win seventh gold," AP, ESPN.com, 11/25/08
119	Changingminds.org; deltabravo.net
120	positivityblog.com/index.php/2006/10/27/18-ways-to-improve-your-body-lan-guage, and marcandangel.com/2008/07/07/25-acts-of-body-language-to-avoid
121	"Setting the Stage," Kevin Hogan, Psy.D., Speaker, publication of National Speakers Association, 6/09
126	*The Sir Winston Method: The Five Secrets of Speaking the Language of Leadership*, James Humes, William Morrow and Company, Inc. 1991
129	*Speak Like Churchill, Stand Like Lincoln*, James C. Humes, Three Rivers, 2002
132	*The Charlie Rose Show*, Public Broadcasting System, 1/29/09
139	*Made to Stick*, Dan Heath and Chip Heath, *Fast Company*, 11/08
144	*On Advertising*, David Ogilvy, Vintage Publishing,1983
146	"The Mind of the Negotiator," Deepak Malhotra and Max H. Bazerman, Harvard Business School, articles in Negotiation Newsletter, 8/07
148	Robert Alan Black at www.cre8ng.com
151	*The Location of Culture*, Rutledge, 1994, in Philosophy and Literature, 1998
154	http://en.wikipedia.org/wiki/Gettysburg_Address
157	*Speak Like Churchill, Stand Like Lincoln*, James C. Humes, Three Rivers, 2002
158	"Backpage," *Marketing News*, 2/15/09
159	seniorjournal.com/NEWS/Entertainment/5-06-22TopMovieLines.htm
160	"It's not what you say, it's how you say it," James P.T. Fatt, *Communication World*, 6/99
163	"Less Hulk, More Bruce Lee," Mark Borden, *Fast Company*, 4/07
168	"Spin Your Success: Leadership lessons from a top Hollywood mover and shaker" Best Life Website, 7/08
170	*Mad Men*, American Movie Classics Company LLC, Season 1, Episode 13.
172	actionscript-toolbox.com/quotes/author/Luke-Wilson.html
176	"The Disaster," J.L. August and Sara D. Anderson, *Fast Company*, 11/08

end notes

179   *Speak Like Churchill, Stand Like Lincoln*, James C. Humes, Three Rivers, 2002; *Nigel Holmes on Information Design*, Steven Heller, Jorge Pinto, 2006

184   "Less Hulk, More Bruce Lee," Mark Borden, *Fast Company*, 10/08

188   "Moooi Fabulous," Linda Tischler, *Fast Company*,10/08

188   *It's Not How Good You Are*, Paul Arden, Phaidon Press, Inc., 2003

190   "Moooi Fabulous," Linda Tischler, *Fast Company*,10/08

191   "Mod Men," Wendy Goodman, *New York*, 3/2/09

195   "Winged Victories: The soaring ambition of Santiago Calatrava," Rebecca Mead, *The New Yorker*, 9/01/08

196   *Hello He Lied—and Other Tales from the Hollywood Trenches*, Linda Obst, Broadway Publishing, 1997

218   "How to Fail in Business, a Guide to Success," J. Alex Tarquinio, *The New York Times*, 7/26/08

219   *Eat, Pray, Love*, Elizabeth Gilbert, Penguin, 1/30/07

222   *The Charlie Rose Show*, PBS, 7/23/08

225   "Wise Negotiators Know When to Say 'I'm Sorry,'" Maurice E. Schweitzer, Negotiation newsletter, Harvard Law School, 12/06

226   "Sales and Customer Service Are Just Like Steroids Used in Baseball," Dave Kurlan, omghub.com/SalesDevelopmentBlog, 2/10/09

227   "Wise Negotiators Know When to Say 'I'm Sorry,'" Maurice E. Schweitzer, Negotiation newsletter, Harvard Law School, 12/06

234   "Revving Up Readership," Ann Wylie, WylieComm.com, 2/24/05; "Rewriters block: How to safely usher copy through the approval process," Rich Smith, *PR Tactics*, 2/09

235   Interview by James M. Pagliasotti, *Eye-Level*, a quarterly journal of contemporary visual culture; "Christo Visits the Business (!) School," by Ken Gewertz, Harvard News Office, 4/13/06

237   "Man of Letters: Matthew Carter's life in type design," Alec Wilkinson, *New Yorker*, 12/5/05

239   bishopmoore.org

index

index